The Self-Shaming God
Who Reconciles

The Self-Shaming God Who Reconciles

A Pastoral Response to Abandonment within the Christian Canon

WARNER M. BAILEY

With a Foreword by David J. Gouwens

☙PICKWICK *Publications* • Eugene, Oregon

THE SELF-SHAMING GOD WHO RECONCILES
A Pastoral Response to Abandonment within the Christian Canon

Copyright © 2013 Warner M. Bailey. All rights reserved. Except for brief quotations in critical publications or reviews, no part of this book may be reproduced in any manner without prior written permission from the publisher. Write: Permissions, Wipf and Stock Publishers, 199 W. 8th Ave., Suite 3, Eugene, OR 97401.

Pickwick Publications
An Imprint of Wipf and Stock Publishers
199 W. 8th Ave., Suite 3
Eugene, OR 97401

www.wipfandstock.com

ISBN 13: 978-1-61097-768-5

Cataloguing-in-Publication data:

Bailey, Warner M.

The self-shaming God who reconciles : a pastoral response to abandonment within the Christian canon / Warner M. Bailey ; with a foreword by David J. Gouwens.

xiv + 112 pp. ; 23 cm. Includes bibliographical references.

ISBN 13: 978-1-61097-768-5

1. Bible. O.T. Psalms—Criticism, interpretation, etc. 2. Shame—Religious aspects. 3. Canonical criticism. 4. Pastoral theology. I. Gouwens, David J. II. Title.

BT714 B3 2013

Manufactured in the USA

All Scriptural texts, except as where noted, are reprinted from the Common Bible: New Revised Standard Version Bible, copyright 1989, Division of Christian Education of the National Council of the Churches of Christ in the United States of America. Used by permission. All rights reserved.
Additional citations are reprinted from:

Tanakh: The Holy Scriptures: The New JPS Translation to the Traditional Hebrew Text © 1985 by The Jewish Publication Society, with the permission of the publisher.

The Moffatt Translation of the Bible, 1935, Hodder and Stoughton, with the permission of the publisher.

The New American Bible, revised edition © 2010, 1991, 1986, 1970 Confraternity of Christian Doctrine, Washington, DC and are used by permission of the copyright owner.

The quotation from "The Theology of Death and the Care of the Dying" is reprinted with permission from *Insights: The Faculty Journal of Austin Seminary* 110/1 (1994).

To Mary, my wife

Wise Woman, Loving Companion, Creator of Beauty

Contents

Foreword by David J. Gouwens   xi

Introduction   1

1 Psalms 73–75: A Story of Shame and Vindication   15

2 To Be Shamed, Living beyond Shame   36

3 Shame as a Theological Crisis   50

4 Living Beyond Shame within the Christian Canon   66

5 The Self-Shamed God Who Reconciles: A Contribution to Pastoral Theology and Practice   80

Conclusion: Implications for Ministerial Formation   96

Bibliography   101

Foreword

ONE OF THE MORE hopeful signs in recent theology is the increased attention that biblical scholars, theologians, and pastoral theologians alike now give to the task of reuniting their disciplines after decades if not centuries of fragmentation. That attempt goes by many names in theological education, such as "integration" or "interdisciplinarity." Sometimes that attempt seems facile, at worst nostalgic, attempting to recover a sometimes idealized "pre-modern" past before the loss of innocence brought about by the rise of higher biblical criticism, the academic departmentalization of theology, and the demotion of practical theology into "clergy training." At its best, however, this reintegration offers not only "integrated knowledge," but the possibility of more, a personal reintegration in "wisdom" that engages not only the mind but also the will and the heart. So too, as theologian David F. Ford has cogently argued, a wisdom approach to Scripture, theology, and the practices of ministry attends to the "cries" of the world while at the same time remaining thoroughly theocentric, focused on the "theodrama" of God's engagement with humanity.[1]

In *The Self-Shaming God Who Reconciles*, we see Warner M. Bailey offering us the gift of a wisdom hermeneutic at work. From his long experience in ministry, his theme is a strongly pastoral one, arising from the "cries" of the shamed. How may the church address not only the agonies of guilt and sin, but also experiences of shame, the shame that afflicts both "the victims and the perpetrators of failed risks of trust"—the betrayed (or betraying) spouse, the battered child, the abandoned parent, the "outed" gay person? Do we even have the theological vocabulary for dealing with the shame and the sense of abandonment that afflict so many?

---

1. David F. Ford, *Christian Wisdom*. See especially chapter 2 on "a wisdom interpretation of Scripture," which includes Ford's summary of the theses and maxims for interpretation of the Bible proposed by the Princeton Center of Theological Inquiry's Scripture Project.

This study reveals, however, the often surprising ways in which cries of shame, not only sin, are not peripheral but stand at the heart of the biblical witness, and moreover how the "theodrama" of God's relation to humanity addresses precisely this all-too-human experience of shame and abandonment. Schooled professionally as a biblical scholar with interests in canonical interpretation of the Scriptures, Dr. Bailey explores with care the astounding cries of abandonment and shame directed to the God of covenant in Psalms 73, 74, and 75. He turns then to the theme of shame in the Book of the Twelve, before placing all of these texts in conversation with the New Testament, most notably a Trinitarian reading of the Father's abandonment of the Son in the crucifixion narratives, and "shame" in the "canonical Paul" of Romans, Philippians, and 2 Timothy.

Dr. Bailey fruitfully combines biblical exegesis, constructive theological reflection, and pastoral application, navigating all three disciplines with competence and ease. As a theologian, I am especially struck by his fresh insights into how shame is central to an understanding of the "theodrama" of God's identification with the shamed in the crucifixion and resurrection. Here he draws upon the important work of Reformed theologian Alan E. Lewis on "Holy Saturday," who in turn relies upon Karl Barth, Jürgen Moltmann, Eberhard Jüngel, and Hans Urs von Balthasar. But Bailey's focus upon shame, grounded in his careful exploration of the biblical materials, gives his theological account of the crucifixion and resurrection its own distinctiveness and force, the "theodrama" of "the shamed God who lives beyond shame."

But how does this affect our pastoral practice? A special beauty of this book is the clarity with which Dr. Bailey portrays the utter relevance of this "self-shaming God" for both victims and perpetrators of shame. First, attending to the biblical theme of shame helps us to rethink the doctrine of sin. Too often, he suggests—and in this he is not alone in recent theology—we assume that sin is the only human dilemma that God addresses and heals, but then we are helpless addressing the different dynamics of shame and abandonment. Here appears the wisdom of Dr. Bailey's approach, for second, he portrays—with sensitivity to the complexities and difficulties of the task—how the pastor and indeed the entire congregation may create in its ministries and worship safe space and resources for pastoral care, not only for sinners, but for those who, whether victims or agents of shame, are called to live beyond shame.

Foreword

I began by noting how divinity schools and seminaries in recent years are seeking "integration" of theological study. Dr. Bailey offers in his book's conclusion concrete suggestions for what such reintegrated theological study would look like. Of course, describing such reintegrated theological study is one thing; practicing it is another. That is, however, where this fine book succeeds yet again, for it not only advocates, it displays this integrated wisdom—scripturally grounded, theologically sophisticated, and pastorally relevant.

David J. Gouwens
Professor of Theology
Brite Divinity School

Introduction

Trust is at the heart of healthy relationships. When trust is broken, the victim is made to feel as nothing. The Bible calls this experience of betrayal "to be shamed." When the victim names God as the betrayer, those who exercise pastoral care in the church are faced with a spiritual crisis of major proportions. This book addresses this urgent and complex issue in the church by leading pastors and those who exercise pastoral care through biblical study and theological reflection to insights that strengthen their role in the recovery of both the victims and the perpetrators of betrayal. Central to this recovery is the solidarity of the self-shaming God with both victim and perpetrator.

Pastors have intimate knowledge of the shame that betrayal of trust causes. Examples abound. A spouse's trust is betrayed by the partner's adultery. A child is battered or exploited by a parent or relative. A woman is date-raped. A gay, lesbian, bi-sexual, or transgendered person is "outed" in a humiliating way. A parent is repudiated by a child. A child is abandoned by a parent. An employer is embezzled by a trusted employee. A pensioner is defrauded her pension. A parishioner is taken advantage of by her minister. An older worker is fired shortly before becoming eligible for retirement benefits. A veteran is denied medical benefits. The list can be endless.

As pastors listen to these stories of people whose trust has been betrayed, we hear expressions of embarrassment, of being made to feel as nothing, unworthy or soiled, of anger at ourselves and others for not defending against being taken advantage of, of uncertainty about our ability for good judgment, of fear of risking trust anew, and of the terror of abandonment—to name some of the most common reactions. We hear these stories with their attendant questions of Why? and How could? We search for a way of providing care, healing, and hope.

As a pastor who not only has spent a life-time listening to these stories but also as one who has painfully lived through the experience of betrayal I have sought to understand the betrayal of trust within the context of the Scriptures of the Christian church. I have found that the word most commonly used in the Bible to describe the state of being betrayed is "to be put to shame." The relationship between trust and shame is epitomized in Ps 22:5: "In thee they trusted and were not put to shame." This book investigates shame as the Bible's way of describing what comes over a person who suffers a failed risk of trust. The objective of the book is to provide a biblical and theological foundation for pastoral work with individuals and congregations who have been put to shame.

SCOPE AND METHOD

I have investigated the category of theological shame within the context of the canon of Christian Scripture with studies of Pss 73–75, The Book of the Twelve (the so-called "Minor Prophets"), the crucifixion narratives in the Gospels, and 2 Timothy. In undertaking these investigations, I make use of the insights and tools of the emerging field of canonical criticism. Discussion of differing ideas of the nature and scope of canonical criticism as well as the demonstration of various models of canonical exegesis are generating a large body of scholarship. In the footnotes to my exegesis in the following chapters, I show my appreciation of relevant parts of this field. But in a word, what I am attempting is to interpret Scripture "from within."

I clearly recognize that the biblical text has an origin in history, and I also appreciate the contributions of various types of criticism—historical, form, redaction, and literary—to grasping the meaning of a text. However, as Scripture for the church, the text does not reach its final interpretation through these methods. David Kelsey renders a balanced judgment on the relationship between canonical criticism and earlier methods of interpretation. Canonical criticism "provides one way in which to make constructive theological use of the results of such scholarship. Indeed, part of what it means to read biblical texts in their canonical form and context is to pay special attention to ways in which editors shaped them into the form they had when they were included in the canon."[1] The canonical approach recognizes that the way Scripture has come into its present shape has intentionally ordered the text into an interpretative framework within Scripture itself. Hence, the exegesis of particular texts rests finally on their coordination within this framework. Our investigations, therefore, begin with describing carefully this framework that governs the interpretation. The result is a picture of God who actively engages the conditions that give

---

1. Kelsey, *Eccentric Existence*, 215.

Introduction

rise to erosion of trust and who in Jesus Christ finally opens a way to live beyond shame.

Another aspect of my methodology concerns the context for my study of shame. Readers may be familiar with studies of honor-shame morés of Mediterranean cultures that focus on shame as a sociopsychological measure of human worth.[2] They will see that my approach starts from another perspective, that of relationships—both human and divine—which are covenantally structured.[3] Being put to shame through betrayal of bonds of trust is something different from bearing the brunt of culturally induced shame.[4]

Even so, cultural experience, as best we can make it out, has great usefulness for interpretation. Certainly the experience of *being culturally shamed* contributes profoundly to the experience of *being put to shame*, of being abandoned by trusted partners and made to feel as nothing.

I suspect that the contrast between those who would approach the Biblical text from the shame-culture of the Mediterranean world and those who would work from within the framework of the canon centers on hermeneutics. For example, interpreters who see shame as culturally induced typically present the scandal of a shamed Messiah as a challenge to be surmounted by believers in confessing the content of faith. Shame is the scandal for the reader/believer to overcome. This book's contribution is that it is grounded in a Trinitarian description of God's saving work. The Trinitarian approach of this book emphasizes the admission of the shame of betrayal into the Godhead as the Son is abandoned by the Father who gives up the Son. It is the Spirit who keeps Father and Son together at the moment of extreme separation. The resurrection of Jesus is the Spirit's authentication of their union that survives beyond betrayal. This is the ground of good

---

2. New Testament anthropological studies of shame include Malina and Neyrey, "Honor and Shame," 25–66, and Daube, "Shame Culture," 355–72.

3. Stansell, "Honor and Shame," 94–114, and Olyan, "Honor, Shame, and Covenant Relations," 201–18. Olyan's study is a helpful introduction to the relation of honor and shame to covenantal practices in the ancient Near East. He concentrates on narrative texts. An earlier investigation by Huber, "The Biblical Experience of Shame/Shaming," secured the difference between shame and guilt and showed that the Old Testament was more concerned with shame than guilt. Huber sought to probe the psychological and emotional origins of shame. She argues that shame's principle use is to control and manipulate behavior. While recognizing the many expressions of shame in the Bible, the present study concentrates on the dynamics of shame as the experience of failed expectations grounded in covenantal trust.

4. I thank Gene Boring for engaging me in a conversation that sharpened this point.

news that the one who places trust in Jesus will not be put to shame in a world of hurt and sin!

THE ARC OF INTERPRETATION

The experience of being put to shame by another is painful and isolating. But its degrading effects are not confined within the human community. Being put to shame by another human being very often is the catalyst for believing that we have been abandoned by God—that God has put us to shame. Certainly the fear of being put to shame by God is what underlies the Psalmist's cry. This terrible prospect is this book's ultimate horizon of reflection. The erosion of trust in God is one of the most serious crises of faith, and this book is offered as a contribution to the work of pastoral caregivers in facing this real and complex issue under the Word of God. I will refer to this experience of being put to shame by God as, alternatively, theological shame or believer's shame.

Pastoral work is only completed, however, when the betrayer is addressed, called to accountability, and invited to repent. This pastoral work is difficult, daunting, and fraught with risk. Yet the evangelistic mission of the church demands that we not shirk this opportunity. I wrestle with this vexing question as well in order to present a global vision of the pastoral care of the shamed and the shamer.

Such a vision demands a robust theological foundation that is based in the canonical Scriptures of the Christian church. This base is prepared in chapter 1 with exegesis of Pss 73–75. I make the case that these psalms have been canonically ordered to play a keystone role in the movement of the entire Psalter. Their canonical ordering permits an investigation of fruitful interactions between them. As we hear these "triplet" psalms through the hermeneutic prism of Pss 1–2, we uncover the issue of theological shame. The threat of this shame to Israel's ongoing life with God provides the context that highlights God's response to it.

In chapter 2, we move from the close readings of these psalms in the context of the Psalter to a synthetic assessment of their content in the Hebrew Bible. The crisis of humans experiencing betrayal by God is set against the experiences of humans betraying humans as recounted in 1–2 Samuel and instances in Isaiah, Jeremiah, and Hosea of the divine pathos of God being betrayed by humans. This larger context underscores the bedrock of covenantal trust against which theological shame is reacting.

Introduction

In chapter 3, we turn our attention to the relationship of Ps 73 and Mal 3:13–18. We study this relationship under the rubric that Malachi and the Psalms form a "seam" between the major blocks of Law-Prophets and the Writings. The Law-Prophets we take as setting forth the basic "grammar" of the Old Testament with the Writings functioning as a reflection upon them. Our investigation of the way Ps 73 comments upon Mal 3 opens up the study of shame in the Book of the Twelve. Befuddled believers struggle to live faithfully in the midst of pressure to lapse into moral cynicism. Within the Book of the Twelve we see snapshots of faithful living amidst conditions that produce theological shame.

By studying instances of the expression of theological shame throughout the Book of the Twelve, it becomes apparent that the division of the Prophets closes with shame as an unsettled question, provoking a rare disclosure of God's stake in the crisis. The use of the self-designation formula (Exod 34:6–7) in strategic places in the Book of the Twelve underscores the integrity of God confronting conditions that threaten that integrity. Because the Book of the Twelve and the Psalms form the "seam" between the Prophets and the Writings, the striking association between Mal 3:13—4:6 and Ps 73 shows how the Psalter can serve as a reflection upon the unsettled question of shame that closes out the Prophets.

In chapter 4, we describe the function of theological shame in the New Testament and sketch the associated canonical conversation between the two testaments. We proceed next to a constructive proposal that sets the shame of the crucifixion and the Father's abandonment of the Son in a Trinitarian matrix. The reunion of Father and Son under the power of the Spirit in the resurrection shows the triumph of God over shame and prepares for the apostolic preaching of the promise that the one who trusts in Jesus will not be put to shame. This theological proposal gives rise to the book's title, *The Self-Shaming God Who Reconciles*.[5] Our New Testament survey closes with the witness of the "canonical Paul" living beyond shame drawn from texts in Romans, Philippians and 2 Timothy.

Using the insights from biblical exegesis refracted through constructive theological reflection, chapter 5 moves the discussion to three foci that can inform and assist pastoral leadership: (1) the pastoral support of both victims and perpetrators of failed risks of trust, (2) the congregational

---

5. This project is a contribution to the discipline of biblical theology construed as the interplay between exegetical and systematic thinking. See Miller, "Theology from Below," 270–301.

setting of the pastoral care of the shamed, and (3) the activity of worship in relationship to living beyond shame.

Pastoral Care

When offering support to persons who have been violated by someone they trusted, pastors can invoke the presence of the self-shamed God in Jesus, abandoned by the Father, as a rock of solidarity. Within the context of solidarity, the pastor can witness to the Spirit's power that makes possible the self-shamed God to live in Jesus beyond shame and proclaim that power as a hope for the shamed one to live beyond shame into renewed trust.

When offering support to persons who have violated someone's trust, pastors can invoke the presence of the self-shaming God who in the Father puts the Son to shame. Pastors can proclaim this self-shaming God as the refuge of all who despitefully use a victim, this God who makes company with the shamers and shares in their judgment. In solidarity with the self-shaming God, those who bear the judgment of trampling upon trust may hear the Spirit calling them to a new life of keeping faith.

Thus the God who knows and bears shame is the center of reconciliation between the shamed and the perpetrators. This reconciliation must be approached with care. It can take various forms. In all circumstances pastors are commissioned to witness to the God who draws shame into the bosom of the divine family and lets it do its worst so that God can win for the world's sake a way beyond shame and offer that way as a gift of grace.

Congregational Care

This pastoral work is difficult and is most effective when delivered in the context of the congregation. Realism suggests that an outbreak of shame threatens the bonds of trust that live at the heart of congregational fellowship and mission. Pastors will place the life of their congregation inside the story of the fractured Trinitarian family of God and will testify to the role of the Spirit who keeps the Father and the Son in union even in their mutual shame and calls them to new life. Pastors will present this testimony as the warrant for hope in the power of renewal of their congregation and will dare to attempt to keep the shamed one and perpetrators inside the community's circle of power.

Worship

Worship witnesses to the self-shaming God who reconciles. Praise indicates that the paralyzing burden of shame is released. Praise voices confidence in and recommitment to God's sovereign way with the world. As praise celebrates the reasserting of the two-ways formula, praise establishes the foundation for ethics.

Pastors will always be alive to instances of deep and searching awareness of the self that occur as the result of going through an opening to life beyond shame. These moments of awareness ought to be celebrated with praise. The Bible shows that worship which helps recall history that is reduced to its sacred core and worship that dramatizes a preview of the future victory will be an instrument of God's saving of the shamed.

SHAME AS A THEME OF PASTORAL THEOLOGY

It may be helpful to situate this book within the larger field of pastoral theology and care. In the past two decades, pastoral theologians have rediscovered shame as a powerful conditioner of human behavior. This has happened largely in response to the recognition of the difference between shame and guilt. Donald Capps, writing about sin, exemplifies this change in perspective.

> In our times, we are much more likely to experience this "wrongfulness" according to shame, rather than guilt, dynamics. Thus, to speak meaningfully and relevantly about sin, we have to relate sin to the experience of shame—not only, not even primarily, to the experience of guilt. Obviously this will involve a reformulation of our theology of sin, a reformulation that is so deep and extensive that it calls for a fundamental change in our theological paradigm . . . no one has addressed in a systematic way the specific problem of how to reflect on sin within a cultural milieu in which shame, not guilt, is the predominant experience, the more deeply felt emotion.[6]

Because pastoral theologians work collaboratively with psychological theory, shame is typically treated as a phenomenon that is ontological and self-referencing. So, Capps states that "Guilt arises in experience from failing to meet the expectations, real or perceived, of others, shame is felt when the self has failed to attain its own goals, when the realization occurs that

---

6. Capps, *The Depleted Self*, 3. See also Albers, *Shame*, 22.

the self is incapable of achieving its ambitions. The person who is hurt or damaged by this assessment is not another person, but the self. The typical effects of such overwhelming shame are depletion, hollowness, and unfulfilled hunger."[7]

Jill McNish maintains that pervasive shame stands in "the tension that exists between longing for union with others, with society, with God, and the longing for individuation and the living out of one's own 'true' and creative self."[8]

Various kinds of shame can be identified and their interactions described. Robert Albers distinguishes between healthy shame and unhealthy shame, between discretionary shame and disgrace shame.[9] McNish uses psychoanalysis and personality theory to argue that shame is a means of revelation of God and the self.[10]

It should be apparent that our investigation begins from a different perspective. It offers a model of pastoral practice that begins with biblical exegesis in a canonical setting of texts that speak of shame and proceeds to subject this exegesis to theological reflection before suggesting several outcomes for the life and ministry of the congregation. While acknowledging the deeply probing work of pastoral theologians who investigate shame from the perspective of psychology, it is helpful to point out areas where our work from a different perspective makes a new contribution.

The issues that are at the heart of this book speak to the experience of shame as abandonment, betrayal and failed risk. The axis around which we proceed is trust-betrayal-shame. This fundamentally moves our discussion out of the realm of shame as ontological and self-referencing. Whereas pastoral theologians typically appeal to claims that shame is creation-based, we come at shame from the perspective of trust and betrayed expectations. This perspective opens the reader to notions of covenant and obedience. The shame we investigate is not generated by the self but is visited upon the self through the actions of a trusted other. Consequently, our approach maintains a dynamic tension between shame and guilt, fastening the guilt upon the one who puts someone to shame through betrayal. Judgment

---

7. Capps, *The Depleted Self*, 34.

8. McNish, *Transforming Shame*, 142. See other examples in Capps, *The Depleted Self*, 34; Smedes, *Shame and Grace*, ix; Nathanson, *Shame and Pride*, 19.

9. Albers, *Shame*, 10–14; Smedes, *Shame and Grace*, ix.

10. McNish, *Transforming Shame*, 35, 51–52, 190–94.

upon the guilty comes in the form of putting the guilty to shame by showing the falseness of what the guilty had put their trust.

In standard treatments of shame from a pastoral perspective "innocent shame" is underdeveloped,[11] and issues of trust and abandonment are treated as a subset of a larger genus of "disgrace shame."[12] Our book makes the claim that the experience of shame as betrayal is central to pastoral care and that understanding this experience within the orb of biblical exegesis and theological reflection highlights the healing of shame that can happen in the Christian community.

Furthermore, God as one who is charged with putting the innocent to shame does not figure decisively where shame is interpreted from an anthropological premise. Nor does the working out within the Trinity of a resolution of shame as abandonment play a foundational role. Instead, pastoral theologians are likely to appeal to an idealized picture of God who underscores the goodness of everybody against the assaults of shame.[13]

The role Jesus plays in typical pastoral approaches to shame is to show solidarity with those who suffer the experience of being failed persons. His cross is conclusive evidence of his failure, and his resurrection provides a pathway out of the shame of failure.[14] Large assumptions are made about Jesus' self-consciousness that the gospel texts have difficulty supporting.

Our approach is based on a closer reading of biblical texts. In that sense it has points of convergence with other appeals to the Bible from pastoral theologians such as Donald Capps (*Biblical Approaches to Pastoral Counseling*) and William B. Oglesby Jr. (*Biblical Themes for Pastoral Care*). However, our approaches differ radically. Capps works out a model of pastoral counseling based on form-criticism of texts while Oglesby pursues a tradition-history approach. Only Capps makes major use of the psalms of lament, restricting himself to their relationship to the grieving process, but he does not develop the experiences of the shame of betrayal they convey. My tack is to proceed from exegesis to synthesis to theological reflection

---

11. Smedes, *Shame and Grace,* 38, speaks of "undeserved shame" as "a false message from our false self." Capps, *The Depleted Self,* 35, describes narcissists as "victims of emotional deprivations that are most certainly undeserved."

12. McNish, *Transforming Shame,* 36–38.

13. See, for example, the use McNish, *Transforming Shame,* 128, makes of the theology of Paul Tillich and the appeal of Albers, *Shame,* 118–19 to the *imago Dei*.

14. Albers, *Shame,* 102–3; McNish, *Transforming Shame,* 12, 15, 16, 20, 166, 167, 168–73; Capps, *The Depleted Self,* 98.

before drawing inferences for pastoral leadership that impinges on care of individuals, congregations, ethics and worship.[15]

We acknowledge in chapter 5 many valuable insights that pastoral theology provides, particularly in the care of the shamed and the one who puts to shame. Yet, we hope to advance the understanding of this deeply felt emotion from a fresh perspective.

Shame and Trauma

More helpful in the direction of what we are doing are insights offered through the hard work of psychiatrists and therapists in understanding and treating psychological effects of traumatic events. Psychiatrist Judith Lewis Herman locates trauma along the expectations-betrayal-shame axis we are exploring. "Traumatic events call into question basic human relationships. They breach the attachments of family, friendship, love, and community. They shatter the construction of the self that is formed and sustained in relation to others. They undermine the belief systems that give meaning to human experience. They violate the victim's faith in a natural or divine order and case the victim into a state of existential crisis."[16]

Trauma theory supports the treatment of rape survivors and combat veterans, of battered women and political prisoners, of victims of child abuse and survivors of concentration camps. Many of the themes we encounter in the biblical notion of shame play crucial roles in understanding psychological trauma: betrayal of trust, abandonment, loss of faith, nothingness.[17] Herman incisively points out that "Shame is a response to helplessness, the violation of bodily integrity, and the indignity suffered in the eyes of another person."[18]

Likewise, life beyond shame in the Bible and the recovery from traumatic injury share many of the same traits: restoring of relationships, a renewed sense of faith, and approaching life with praise and awe.[19] Both lines of inquiry validate the crucial role of the community in the healing

---

15. In that sense, this book shares formal similarities to Billman and Migliore, *Rachel's Cry*.

16. Herman, *Trauma and Recovery*, 51 and van der Kolk et al., *Traumatic Stress*.

17. See Herman, *Trauma and Recovery*, on betrayal of trust, 55, 100; on abandonment, 52, 92; on loss of faith, 94; on nothingness, 94.

18. Ibid., 53.

19. Ibid., on restoring of relationships, 3, 154; on a renewed sense of faith, 153, 196; and on approaching life with praise and awe, 212.

of the shamed person.²⁰ In the restoration of trust, Herman underscores the requirement of the therapist's costly witness to the unburdening of the victim's shame of being traumatized.²¹

Perhaps the most fruitful theological appreciation of trauma theory comes from Serene Jones' collection of essays, *Trauma and Grace: Theology in a Ruptured World*. Drawn from her experience in ministering to persons with post-traumatic stress syndrome and her life within a support group of women who have suffered a miscarriage, Jones fastens on the power of the Bible's story to resonate with damaged imaginations in a healing way.²² She sketches ways the congregation can provide this restoration of a traumatized imagination through embodying healing through prayer, song and gesture.²³ Jones' interpretation of Calvin's commentary on the psalms as a sustained response to a community's experience of the shame of betrayal is particularly germane to the argument of this book.²⁴

The findings of trauma theory provide a fruitful interchange with theological shame from the opposite perspective as well: that of the perpetrator of trauma. David J. Livingston, who works as a therapist with batterers, describes how necessary is the community setting for the pastoral care of the shamers, not only for the protection of the ones violated but just as critically for the healing of the violator: "If the man feels that he has other people who care about his well-being and understand the difficulty of losing his partner and children, he may be more likely to succeed in his journey toward nonviolence. The church community has a primary responsibility to assure the batterer that he remains connected to a caring community of support. This community will not only support him but also hold him responsible to the principles found within the gospel of love and respect."²⁵

Livingston calls his model of the recovery process of the violator "reconciliation." This nomenclature is unfortunate because it automatically implies reunion, which can be interpreted as "forgive and forget." Livingston cautions heavily against this implication and argues for the term in its root meaning of *re-concilium*, renewed awareness of the violator of his own

---

20. Ibid., 70, 133. On the impact of trauma on community, see Jones, "Emmaus Witnessing," 117.

21. Herman, *Trauma and Recovery*, 138.

22. Jones, *Trauma and Grace*, 20–21, 49, 53–54.

23. Ibid., 52, 64.

24. Ibid., 48.

25. Livingston, *Healing Violent Men*, 23.

capacity to be loved by God, by others, and by himself and re-entry into the larger community.[26] Drawing on the theology of Thomas Aquinas, he charts a model of reconciliation proceeding from Contrition through Confession and Satisfaction before reaching Absolution.[27]

Against Herman's generic model for the recovery process of violated persons (establishing safety, reconstructing the trauma story, and restoring the connection between survivors and their community)[28] Livingston's chart of recovery of the violator appears as a mirror image. Both models have restoration to community as the desired goal, but it is worth noting Livingston's careful parsing of the contours of this restoration.

> Healing in the interhuman sphere involves the perpetrator's relinquishing his desire to control or punish his partner and possibly his partner's capacity to forgive him. Yet, reconciliation, if it is to address the violating within the interhuman sphere, must also address the anger and resentment of the survivor of violence. To heal this resentment does not involve forgetting the violation, but creating the conditions for the survivor's being able to wish the well-being of the penitent batterer.[29]
>
> It is not the role of church leaders and the church community to demand that the violated forgive the violator. Instead it is the community's task to create an environment in which both violator and violated may begin the healing process, which may at some point include forgiveness . . . Reconciliation is the first step and it must be viewed as enough.[30]

Both Livingston and Herman, operating from complementary aspects of trauma theory, provide material for fruitful reflection in chapter 5 in the discussion of the pastoral care of the shamed and shamer.

This study originated with a presentation to regional church leaders on the subject of the demands and hopes of congregational leadership. Ps 73 seemed to be a fruitful place to ground my thoughts. In preparation I was led to the intriguing insight by Walter Zimmerli of its close relationship with Pss 74 and 75. Thus the groundwork was prepared for a full-blown investigation. Along the way, I have profited from sharing various stages

---

26. Ibid., 82.
27. Ibid., 69–80.
28. Herman, *Trauma and Recovery*, 3.
29. Livingston, *Healing Violent Men*, 82.
30. Ibid., 92. See also the helpful guidance on ministry with violent men offered by Cooper-White, *The Cry of Tamar*, 206–28.

Introduction

of its development with church groups and colleagues, both academics and pastors. The extensive footnotes express my indebtedness to exegetes, systematic theologians and pastoral theologians. I express special thanks to colleagues: the late Andrew Lester, Alan Cole, David Gouwens, Michael Jinkins and Cynthia Rigby for conversations that have both challenged and encouraged. Presenting before a peer reading group and teaching a graduate seminar provided opportunities for critical reflection and shaping.

This book reflects my commitment to enhancing the vitality of the church through educating a leadership that takes seriously the mutual indwelling of exegesis, theological reflection and praxis. In a Conclusion, I offer observations on how theological education could better shape ministerial students for the tweny-first century.

1

Psalms 73–75
A Story of Shame and Vindication

The Bible is the authoritative witness to the self-shaming God who reconciles. We begin with listening carefully to biblical texts for testimony to this God. Guided by this testimony, we will be able to think constructively in proposing a theology upon which pastoral leadership can be described.

In an article for the G. Ernest Wright *Festschrift* published in 1976, Brevard S. Childs gave an account of the modern study of the Psalms. In his reflections upon the diminishing exegetical returns of form-critical and tradition-historical approaches and his probing for newer methods and assumptions, Childs forecast what has become a new generation of Psalms interpretation. In particular, Childs pointed to several issues that held promise of fruitful results from further investigation:

1. How the psalms were finally collected and given their present shape, giving special attention to the significance for reinterpretation of the positioning of individual psalms (especially royal psalms) within the various collections.

2. How older psalms achieved a normative character and were reused in later psalms, the significance of which gives rise to the issue of canon.

3. How psalms that once were accessible through the cult have been given a new setting that makes them serve later generations in fresh ways.

Collectively these issues suggested a new appreciation of the canonical form of the Psalter. Childs concluded his reflections with this invitation, "I would argue that the need for taking seriously the canonical form of the Psalter would greatly aid in making use of the psalms in the life of the

Christian Church. Such a move would not disregard the historical dimensions of the Psalter but would attempt to profit from the shaping that the final redactors gave the older material to transform traditional poetry into Sacred Scripture for the later generations of the faithful."[1]

For the past thirty years Child's invitation has called forth a wealth of scholarship on which this present study rests.[2] Investigators in this country such as Walter Brueggemann, Patrick Miller, James Mays, Gerald Sheppard, J. Clinton McCann Jr., and Gerald H. Wilson have set the terms for a new synthesis for study of the Psalter. By 1992, the shape of this new synthesis had emerged with sufficient clarity that the editors of *Interpretation* devoted their April issue to its demonstration (where articles by McCann and Wilson are particularly helpful).

It is not our purpose to rehearse the details of this new formulation.[3] For our purposes, the following outline of it suffices to situate our subject, the interpretation of Pss 73–75 for the life of the Christian Church.

In basic outline, it is well known that the final redactors of the Psalter's 150 psalms set them into five books, each section concluding with a doxology. McCann and Wilson especially have noticed that the psalms in each book have differing views of the Davidic monarchy. Books I and II (Pss 1–72) contain psalms that present a positive picture of the Davidic monarchy, but Book III (Pss 73–89) ushers in a more negative presentation of the stability of the monarchy.[4] The shapers of Book III arranged psalms to cause this negative picture to become more intense, ending with the final debacle of the monarchy in Ps 89.[5] Books IV and V (Pss 90–150) contain psalms that have the common theme of God as King and look forward to the establishment of the kingship of God in the future, independent of the Davidic monarchy. As will be shown later in this study, this ordering of psalms sets up for Israel a trajectory toward a future hope that issues in an eschatological stamp placed on the final form of the Psalter.[6]

---

1. Childs, "Reflections," 378.
2. For a survey of canonical interpretation on the psalms, see Cole, *Shape and Message*, 9–14.
3. See Wenham, "Towards a Canonical Reading," 333–51.
4. Wilson, "Use of Royal Psalms," 85–94.
5. Clifford, "Psalm 89," 35–47.
6. Wilson, *The Editing*. The shaping of the Psalter has drawn the interest of a large group of scholars. See McCann, "Books I–III," and Vincent, "Shape of the Psalter," 61–82; Nasuti, "Interpretive Significance," 311–39, and Wilson, "King, Messiah," 391–406.

This analysis of the changing Davidic cast of the Psalter's books is grounded in the insight that the so-called royal psalms appear in strategic locations in the progression of the Psalter. As Gerald Wilson has so effectively shown, the placement of the royal Psalms 2, 72, and 89 in the Psalter is critical in understanding the dynamics of the movement of thought from beginning to end. These psalms are placed strategically at the seams of Books I, II, and III. Psalm 2 comes at the beginning of the Psalter. Indeed some scholars believe that it was the first psalm in an earlier collection. Gerald Sheppard has shown the links between Pss 1 and 2, and a case can be made for taking this pair of linked psalms as the composite beginning of Books I–II in which a faith community orients itself on obedience and Davidic rule under God's overlordship.[7] Psalm 72 comes at the end of Book II, and functions as the epitome of this position. Psalm 89, which recounts the wholesale destruction of the monarchy, comes at the end of Book III.

This overarching hypothesis was strengthened further by studies by Mays, Miller, and Sheppard who argued for the hermeneutical priority of Ps 1 with its emphasis on instruction in torah-piety as the prism through which the entire Psalter was to be appreciated.[8] Brueggemann brought this insight to a holistic conclusion by pairing Ps 150 with Ps 1, suggesting that the two "book-ends" chart a trajectory of the life of faith from obedience to praise. This path moves through individual psalms by the stages of orientation, disorientation and re-orientation.[9]

By 1996, twenty years after Child's invitation, the investigation into the canonical shape of the Psalter had gained sufficient consensus for Brueggemann and Miller to issue this summary judgment: "As the study of the 'canonical shape' of the book of Psalms emerges, two observations appear to be settled and definitional to the enterprise. First, the placement of psalms at the 'seams', between the several 'books of the Psalter', is particularly important. Secondly, the themes of torah ('torah piety') and kingship are peculiarly important for the shaping and interpretive intention of the Psalter. Clues can be spotted by the appearance and placement of these themes that the Psalter is to be read with attention to these two accents."[10] This study is grounded upon these fundamental insights.

---

7. Sheppard, "Psalms," 49–98. See further McCann, "Shape of Book I," 341–43.

8. Miller, "The Beginning of the Psalter," 83–92; Mays, "The Place of the Torah-Psalms," 3–12; Mays, "The Question of Context," 14–20.

9. Brueggemann, "Bounded by Obedience and Praise," 80–91.

10. Bruegemann and Miller, "Psalm 73," 45. The magisterial commentary of Hossfeld and Zenger, *Psalms 2*, is grounded in this approach.

INTRODUCTION TO PSALMS 73, 74, AND 75

The affinity of Pss 73–75 was noticed by Walther Zimmerli in his study of *Zwillingspsalmen*.[11] He drew attention to the presence of מַשֻּׁאוֹת ("ruins" or "deceptions") in Ps 73:18 and 74:3 as the only two plural occurrences in the Hebrew Bible, and the *Stichwort* מוֹעֵד ("appointed time/place") in Pss 74:4, 8, and 75:2 (Heb). As this study progresses, we offer additional evidence of a thoughtful redactive process that binds together these psalms into a programmatic statement.

What our investigation has uncovered is that Pss 73–75 stand as an overture to the entire corpus of Books III–V.[12] By careful analysis of linguistic, literary, and thematic relationships between Pss 73–75 we show that the framers of the Psalter use these psalms as a marker right at the mid-point of the Psalter that foreshadows the progression of the theology of the Psalter through the remainder of the corpus. This marker answers succinctly a crisis of faith, reflected in the progression of these three psalms, specifically the crisis of shame brought about by a theological perception. The perception is that God has withdrawn God's presence from the speaker's life. God is addressed as defaulting on the speaker's repose of trust in God. This crisis of faith intensifies throughout the progression of the psalms of Book III, which reflect the collapse of the claims of a David/Zion theology. Books IV and V are arranged to respond to this crisis with renewed affirmation of God's kingship.

The community that took up these keystone psalms thus was given a way to confront the question of theodicy with its attendant affection of theological shame and to resolve both the question and the affection into a place of renewed confidence as the community listened to a divine promise to save.

---

11. Zimmerli, "Zwillingspsalmen," 105–12. For another example of the interpretation of a Zwillingspsalmen see deClassé-Walford, "Intertextual Reading," 139–52.

12. McCann, "Books I–III," 95ff. revived interest in linking Pss 73–74 as the beginning of a pattern of alternating expressions of lament and hope throughout the Asaph collection in Book III. He draws upon the tradition-history studies of Nasuti, *Tradition History*, 188–91, in maintaining that "praise psalms of the Asaphites did not make it into the Psalter along with Psalms 50, 73–83," 106. This overlooks the unique place of Ps 75 as a praise song and its crucial place and linkage to Pss 73–74.

Psalms 73–75

LISTENING TO PSALM 73

In his path-breaking article on the Psalms as canon, Walter Brueggemann gives special attention to Psalm 73 and its unique position of opening Book III of the Psalter.

> My argument concerning the canonical function of Psalm 73 is indeed distinctive and performs a function for Books III–V not unlike that of Psalm 1 for Books I–II. That is, Psalm 73 reiterates the thesis of Psalm 1 and then enters into dispute with that thesis. On the other hand, the stance taken by Psalm 73, of affirmation and then dispute, is a stance taken over and over again in the Psalter. Thus I suggest that Psalm 73 assumes a paradigmatic function, providing a normative example of the frequently reiterated, re-enacted argument made in the Psalter concerning, (a) the reliability of God's *ḥesed*, (b) the doubting of that *ḥesed*, and (c) the ultimate embrace of it in trust and confidence.[13]

To use Brueggemann's very helpful schematic of the movement within individual psalms from orientation through disorientation to reorientation,[14] Psalm 73 marks the beginning of the disorientation section (Book III) of the entire Psalter as the orienting position of Books I and II collapses.[15]

Psalm 73 confronts the breakdown of the confident promises of Ps 1 that "the Lord knows the way of the righteous, but the way of the wicked

---

13. "Bounded by Obedience and Praise," 80–81.

14. "Psalms and the Life of Faith," 3–32. Brueggemann's approach, linking Ps 73 with the theological position stamped at the beginning of the Psalter, shifts the discussion of the function of the Asaph collection away from the search for a putative historical setting and tradition-history locale. See McCann, "Books I–III," 105–6; and Nasuti, *Tradition History*, 161–97. In this sense, Brueggemann takes seriously the final form of the Psalter.

15. In 1996, Brueggemann together with Patrick D. Miller published further discussion of Ps 73 as a canonical marker (fn. 10). They advanced the thesis that the speaker of the psalm is "intended to be the king, the model and embodiment of genuine faith" (48). Central to this interpretation is their positing a relationship of this psalm to Pss 15–24 (see further Miller, "Kingship"). But Brueggemann and Miller note that their conclusions do not advance our understanding of the function of Ps 73 as canonical marker within the crucially placed Book III. "We have at this point no suggestion of an organizing principle for Book III, except to notice that Psalms 73 and 89 bracket a corpus with a heavy emphasis upon Zion and David" (52). The most they can say is that the psalm begins Book III by describing the alternatives of autonomy or piety that will inform the pilgrimage of faith to its disastrous conclusion in Ps 89. We affirm this paradigmatic function of Ps 73, but, we suggest that it is better to understand the psalm in close connection with the two psalms that follow it rather than interpreting it against a royal background.

shall perish."[16] While Ps 1:3 maintains of the righteous, "In all that he does, he prospers," the speaker of Ps 73 admits to disorienting envy "when I saw the prosperity of the wicked" (v.3).

However, this is not the only issue Ps 73 disputes. Its context is prepared by Ps 72, a psalm in which the claims of the Davidic monarchy reach their zenith and by the linkage of Ps 2 with Ps 1 as the composite beginning of Books I–II. So while Ps 73 ushers in Book III by raising a threat to the theological position of Ps 1, the ground is prepared for a linked threat to the monarchy by (1) the implication of Ps 2 through Ps 73's dispute with the promises of Ps 1 and (2) the context of Ps 72 as a positive statement of David's rule.

Brueggemann outlines the crisis facing the speaker of Ps 73. On one side some hold that purity of heart must yield tangible blessings, the corollary being that misfortune indicates moral failure.[17] However, others experience material blessings from overt exploitation, under the belief that God is impotent.[18] The failure of "delight in the law" to bring for the psalmist prosperity "in all that they do" (Ps 1:2–3) coupled with seeing exploiters enjoying ill-gotten prosperity makes the speaker cry, "All in vain have I kept my heart pure and washed my hands in innocence"(v. 13). Thus does Ps 73 enter into a serious dispute with the torah claims of Ps 1 and, by proxy, with the Davidic claims of Ps 2.

The phrase "all in vain" (אַךְ־רִיק) underscores more than the pathos of the speaker's complaint. It also gestures to a condition of shame that exacerbates the speaker's troubles. Shame is a powerful component of self-understanding in the Bible.[19] The shame of Ps 73 does not result from the speaker's own failed risk.[20] Rather, it is occasioned by the speaker's having

16. Brueggemann, "The Cunning Little Secret."

17. For links between Ps 73 and Job, see Luyten, "Psalm 73," 59–81. Yet, Paul Ricoeur, "Lamentation as Prayer," 212, makes an important distinction between psalms of lamentation and wisdom thinking. While both genres ask the question *why?* to God, a "frontier . . . separates a why held within the bounds of prayer from a why that frees itself from this framework and enters into the space of gravitation of speculation concerning God. So long as interrogation remains included within the boundaries of an address to God, it conserves a more 'existential' than speculative aspect."

18. Bruegemann, "The Cunning Little Secret."

19. This theme receives expanded treatment in chapter 2. See for bibliography Odell, "The Inversion of Shame,"101–12. Further bibliography may be found in Lapsley, "Shame and Self-Knowledge," 143–73.

20. The phrase אַךְ־רִיק is unique as far as I can tell to the Old Testament. For similar expressions of shame over failed ventures see David's self-castigation in 1 Sam 25:21 and

misplaced trust in God who fails to be loyal.[21] Margaret Odell points to this experience of shame in the psalms.

> The complaint psalms reflect an analogous understanding of the dynamics of the divine-human relationship. In these psalms, the plea not to be put to shame is often combined with the psalmist's confession that he has put his trust in God (Pss 25:2, 20; 31:2). The plea, 'I have trusted in you; let me not be put to shame,' appeals to God to honor the petitioner's dependence. If the psalmist should experience distress, sickness or the scorn of his community, then that is because God has failed him . . . It is also worth noting that the expression of shame is the opposite of what we would consider the feeling of unworthiness; rather, it is the expression of an individual's outrage that others do not acknowledge and respond to his or her claims.[22]

In Ps 73 shame, indicated by "all in vain," occurs when the speaker experiences God's disloyalty in not responding with prosperity to behavior that comes from innocent hands and a clean heart.

As this study progresses we will see how these three psalms are bound in a unity through the themes of (1) the state of shame brought about by God's experienced disloyalty, (2) the psalmist's dealing with shame by expressing outrage, complaint, and petition surrounding God's absence, and (3) God's response through the transference of shame from the petitioner to the enemies of God. Psalm 73 emphasizes themes one and three. Psalm 74 concentrates on theme two. Psalm 75, while presupposing themes one and two, highlights theme three.

J. Clinton McCann has demonstrated that in Ps 73 the movement from crisis to a resolution pivots around v. 15, which speaks of a powerful claim of a faith community upon the speaker.[23] The tug of the "circle of your children" draws the disputing speaker back into the sanctuary where God vouchsafes a revelation of nearness. The psalm forcefully contrasts

---

the Servant's negative self-evaluation in Isa 49:4. These texts are explored more fully in chapter 2.

21. Odell, "The Inversion of Shame," 104.

22. Ibid., 104–5. See Brueggemann, *Theology*, 467. Ps 44:8–9 contrasts vividly two basic experiences of Israel's relationship with God. In v. 8 the speaker enthusiastically embraces boasting in God and giving thanks, but in v. 9 God is accused of shaming the speaker by the withdrawal of God's presence through not having gone out with Israel's armies.

23. I am indebted to McCann for this insight. See his "Psalm 73," 247–57.

The Self-Shaming God Who Reconciles

the claims of the "pure in heart" (v. 1) with the experience of the speaker self-described as one "pricked in heart" (v. 21). The experience in the sanctuary shows the psalmist that the "good" (v. 1) claimed by the (so-called) "pure in heart" is actually God's nearness (v. 28) to one who was "pricked in heart." Held by God's hand (v. 23) in the sanctuary the psalmist sees the world rightly. Safety, clarity, confidence, overflowing gratitude flood in and sweep out envy, self-pity, shame and cynicism (vv. 23–27). Congruently, the psalmist now can review the prior experience of shame as a time of profound disorientation and froward behavior and marvel that this episode was not repulsive to God.[24]

Similarly, in the temple God shows the psalmist the transference of shame to the arrogant and wicked (vv. 18–19). God lifts the shame that came over the psalmist from experiencing what was thought to be God's ill-founded loyalty, and God settles that shame in judgment upon those who now see that confidence in themselves was fatally ill founded. Thus the placing of the wicked in slippery places endorses the verdict of the conclusion of Ps 1 "the wicked shall not stand in the judgment." We shall see similar language in Ps 75.

It is important to note that the sanctuary is the location where the psalmist's world is put to right against the threats posed by those who take the name of God vainly to justify themselves. This location requires us to inquire more carefully into the complex relationship between temple and world. Jon D. Levenson shows that in the ancient Near East, the "Temple is a visible, tangible token of the act of creation, the point of origin of the world, the 'focus' of the universe . . . [The Temple] is the world *in nuce*, and the world is the Temple *in extenso*."[25] Beset by doubts and threats, the speaker of Ps 73 enters the sanctuary and experiences reversal of shame, restoration, and reorientation.

The temple is the concentration of the world created as a place of order upheld by God's presence.[26] Levenson elaborates, "In cult service the individual experiences a world of order; in this service the individual finds a place for his experiences and expectations. The life that the cult promotes is characterized by harmony. The life-threatening forces are separated from this creative sphere of order."[27]

---

24. For a similar expression, see Ps 92:5–9.
25. Levenson, "The Temple," 283, 285.
26. Lindstrom, *Suffering and Sin*, 91–97.
27. Ibid., 93–94.

Psalms 73-75

Temple theology offers access to God as king who sits invisibly on a throne in the temple of Zion as a saving presence among people. By coming to the Temple, humans can directly experience what it means to be taken up into the saving presence of *Deus praesens* (e.g., "I am continually with you; you hold my right hand. You guide me with your counsel" (73:23–24)). There they are presented with what, strictly speaking, belongs only to God (e.g., "God is the rock of my heart and my portion for ever." (v. 26)).[28] This complex relationship between temple, divine presence, and world of order will be an important tool in our explicating the interrelationships of Pss 73-75.

The final verses of Ps 73 offer a summary description of the two contrasting destinies of those who are far and those who are near God. This conclusion follows the pattern of the conclusion of Ps 1 with its description of the "two ways" of the wicked and the righteous. Thus the claims of Ps 1 that center on "delight in the law" receive a fresh confirmation in Ps 73 through its focus upon nearness to God.[29] While the discourse has turned on the claims of torah piety, the linkage with Ps 2 suggests a similar dynamic of disputation with Davidic claims is possible and forthcoming.

Though the crisis of shame is resolved, the architecture of the psalm creates the impression that the resolution is delicate at best.[30] After the title, the particle אך begins Section I of 12 lines (vv. 1–14). This section is divided into a group of 3 lines that describe the plight of the psalmist (vv.1–3) followed by a group of 9 lines beginning with the particle כי describing the prosperity of the wicked (vv.4–14). The particle אך begins Section II of

---

28. Ibid., 95.

29. The teaching of the Two Ways may have originated in Deut 11:26-28, "Behold I set before you this day a blessing and a curse, the blessing if you heed the commandments of the Lord your God, which I command you this day; and the curse, if you shall not heed the commandments of the Lord your God, but turn aside . . . to go after other gods, which you have not known." The formula of the two ways is central to the exhortation of wisdom material. In the Psalter, it occurs mostly in psalms of Books I and II. While appearing frequently as a conclusion to a psalm, it can be found elsewhere, either in tight construction or elaborated as petition, praise, or declarative statement. See for example, 5:4–12; 7:9; 9:6–7; 18:27; 26:9–12; 37:9–11, 17, 18–22, 28, 37–38. The majority of these psalms contain pleas to God to come to the aid of the speaker. Importantly for our study, after Ps 75 it does not appear again until Ps 107, which opens Book V of the Psalter and for the last time in Ps 141:7–8, 10, a plea to God for help against enemies. The formula continues into the Qumran *Manual of Discipline* 3:4 and into the early Christian documents, the *Didache* and the *Epistle of Barnabas*. See especially *Didache* 1:1—5:2

30. See McCann, "Psalm 73." See among many studies, Auffret, "Et moi ," 241–76 and Torunay, "Le Psaume 73," 187-99.

23

5 lines where the resolution of the crisis happens (vv. 15–17). Again, the particle אַךְ begins Section III of 12 lines (vv. 18–28), which is structured to be in chiastic relationship with Section I. A group of 3 lines (vv. 18–20) describes the plight of the wicked followed by a group of 9 lines (vv. 21–28) beginning with the particle כִּי describing the prosperity of the psalmist. This arrangement of completely balanced verses suggests a tensive relationship between crisis and resolution. It is to be expected that the crisis will break-out again and again, making recourse to the sanctuary necessary for reorientation.

AN INNER-TEXTUAL READING OF PSALM 73 AND PSALM 74

Now we are in a position to investigate the way Pss 73–74 speak when read together.[31] Four thematic elements and three formal elements bridge these two psalms.

A major theme is God's sanctuary. Psalm 74 records the lament of a community whose sanctuary has been destroyed by a conquering enemy (v.3). As the community implores God to confront and turn back the enemy, the community reminds God of mighty acts through which God destroyed the mythological monsters of chaos (vv. 13–14) so as to usher in a stable, orderly, secure world.[32] God's royal dominion over the world is symbolized by the two pillars of the temple, the trees of life, indicating entrance into the sphere of life. The presence of the molten sea symbolizes the pacified powers of chaos.[33] The destruction of such symbols may be indicated in vv. 5–6. The community's lament insists that God act again in defense of the sanctuary and the world order of which the sanctuary is an emblem.

Like other nations around it Israel enshrined God's victory over chaos in the temple on Mount Zion, and it is precisely with the destruction of the Temple that Israel's world harmony is fractured. Someone seeking the sanctuary to find reorientation as in Ps 73:17 would be shocked into further disorientation. Joining Ps 74 to Ps 73 now upsets decisively the delicate balance noted in Ps 73 by neutralizing the point where disorientation could

---

31. For studies on the structure of Ps 74, see Sharrock, "Psalm 74," 211–23 and Auffret, "Essai," 129–48.

32. Miller, "The Theological Significance," 229.

33. Lindstrom, *Suffering and Sin*, 94.

be resolved. Now with the sanctuary destroyed, hope is gone for re-gaining stability and harmony.[34]

Closely associated with the theme of sanctuary in the two psalms is the theme of the threat leveled at God's name as uncontested sovereign.[35] In Ps 73, the wicked mock God's omniscience. In Ps 74 God dwells on Mount Zion (v. 2) and the enemy's destruction of the sanctuary is a desecration of the dwelling place of God's name (vv. 7, 10, 18). This scoffing of the impious (vv. 4, 8, 22) joins with the God-mockers in Ps 73:11. By reading Ps 73 in the light of Ps 74, the power of the enemies of God is resurrected, the assault on God's holiness is intensified, and the spiritual crisis of Ps 73 is renewed afresh.

A third theme that both psalms demonstrate is the consequences of this upheaval of world order in increased exploitation of the weak. As those in Ps 73.11 mock God by making God's impotence an encouragement for dominating the weak, so in Ps 74, with the breakdown of the dwelling place of God, the poor, downtrodden and needy are violated (74:20–21).

It is in this context that the fourth theme of shame brought about by ill-founded trust in God occurs. The bewildered psalmist implores God, "Do not deliver the soul of thy dove to the wild beasts . . . have regard for your covenant . . . Do not let the downtrodden be put to shame" (74:19–21).[36] To this plea must be added the imperatives directed toward God "remember" (74:2), "direct" (74:3), "arise" (74:22), and "do not forget" (74:3). The interrogatives, "why?" (74:1 twice and 11 twice) and "how long?" (74:10) give vent to this shame.

---

34. See Hossfeld and Zenger, *Psalms 2*, 250–51. "Since Psalm 73 is an individual's lament (though, of course, set within the horizon of Israel by means of v. 1), and Psalm 74 is a lament of the nation, individual and collective suffering because of God are closely entwined. In addition, Psalm 73 sheds additional interpretive light on the Temple or Zion theology proposed by Psalms 74–76." I differ with Cole, *Shape and Message*, 22–23, who moves backward from Ps 74 to interpret the sanctuaries of Ps 73 already in ruins. Furthermore, Cole (26) identifies the wicked protagonists in Ps 73 as Israel against which the Davidic psalm speaker is contrasted. I take the persons suffering in Ps 74 as innocent sufferers, so that it is illogical to see the Temple's destruction as consequence of wicked Israel. This rules out Cole's contrasting the speaker against the nation. I do not interpret in reverse so that the sanctuaries of Ps 73 are in ruins, but forwards so that the place where resolution happened is no longer available. There are verbal links in Ps 73 with Ps 72 to show how the promises to David are being overturned, but the closing of Ps 72 casts doubt in my judgment on the Davidic character of the speaker in Ps 73.

35. Weiss, *Bible from Within*, 291.

36. McCann, "Books I–III," 100. See further Broyles, *Conflict of Faith and Experience in the Psalms*, 150–54. Broyles studies Ps 74 in isolation.

The Self-Shaming God Who Reconciles

This plea joins with the cry of Ps 73:13 "All in vain have I kept my heart pure and washed my hands in innocence" to produce a compelling representation of the crisis to faith. However Ps 74 adds a new, more frightening dimension. The hand that God extends in Ps 73:23 bringing the speaker a personal confirmation of restored security ("You hold my hand") is now withdrawn in 74:11, allowing the horrible destruction of sanctuary and people.[37] The destruction of the sanctuary can only be possible if God has taken God's protection away (74:11), upsetting the speaker's world of justice and order. God's protection in which the speaker trusted proves ill-founded, leading to the experience of shame and the continuous string of imperatives and interrogatives whose sole purpose is to bring God's protective presence back.[38]

In addition to these four thematic links, Pss 73–74 are joined by three formal elements.

First, both are headed by superscriptions that put them in the collection of the Asaph psalms.[39] David Mitchell has attempted to define the function of this collection in terms of describing an eschatological ingathering where God judges the nations and Israel.[40] McCann and Harry Nasuti posit that the collection was a liturgical resource used in pre- and postexilic times to reflect theologically on God's activity with respect to Zion.[41] Whatever might have been the original function of this collection, we contend that the inclusion of this collection within the canonical framework defined by Pss 1–2 reorients the Asaph psalms toward the goal of resolving the crisis of faith occasioned by the demise of the monarchy and the collapse of the claims of torah piety.

Second, both psalms begin with a three verse introduction that structures what follows. Psalm 73:1–3 introduces the three positions that form

---

37. See Fishbane, "Arm of the Lord," 280–82.

38. Lindstrom, *Suffering and Sin*, 96–97. While Lindstrom confines his investigations to the withdrawal of God's presence in individual complaint psalms, it is interesting to note that the same motif of withdrawal of presence plays itself out in Ps 74 in both national and individual situations.

39. Wilson, "Shaping the Psalter," 73–82. Mitchell in *Message of the Psalter* interprets the Psalms of Asaph as depicting an eschatological ingathering where Israel and the nations are judged. While his interpretation brings forward interesting exegetical points, his hypothesis of an eschatological ingathering full of judgment leads him not to see the inner dynamic between Pss 73–75. He gives no weight to the salvific message of 73 and 75. In this study, we make no claims about the Asaph collection.

40. Mitchell, *Message of the Psalter*, chapter 3.

41. McCann, "Books I–III," 105–6 and fn.12.

the body of the dispute: the "orthodox" position (v. 1), the crisis of the psalmist (v. 2), and the threat of the wicked (v. 3). Psalm 74:1–3 lays out the themes that will be expanded in the three following stanzas: 74:1 upbraids God for inaction, which vv. 18–23 expand; 74:2 calls God to remember the founding acts of the ordering of the world and their enshrinement in Mount Zion, which find elaboration in vv. 12–17; and 74:3 orders God to attend to the crisis of the sanctuary's desecration, which is taken up in vv. 4–11.[42] The chiastic order of this arrangement propels to the beginning of the psalm the unraveling of the speaker's world as demanding immediate attention.

Finally, the placement of Ps 74 now linked to Ps 73, sets the more personal dispute of Ps 73 into the context of a national catastrophe. Book III of the Psalter opens with Ps 73's dispute and closes with the royal Ps 89, which records the community's lament over the destruction of the monarchy. A study of Ps 89 would take us beyond the scope of this book, however it is worth noting that many of motifs of Ps 89 occur in Ps 74, such as God's victory over mythological monsters, God's establishment of world order, the invectives "How long?" "Remember!," the taunting of the enemies, and the description of shame brought about by ill-founded trust in God. The collapse of the Davidic monarchy, while not mentioned in Ps 74, must be kept in view nonetheless in the experience of the desecration of the Temple.

With the cumulative force of these elements, Pss 73–74 launch Book III into the spiritual crisis of shame that attends the collapse of Israel's social, religious, and political life. The speakers of Ps 74 give vent to this crisis as they cry, "Do not deliver the soul of thy dove to the wild beasts . . . have regard for your covenant . . . Do not let the downtrodden be put to shame" (74:19–21). This shame is the result of the intensifying of themes introduced in Ps 73.

PSALMS 73–75 SPEAKING TO EACH OTHER

Psalm 75, also a psalm of Asaph, marks a radical turn in the deepening crisis described by Pss 73–74. The dynamic of this psalm can be caught by noticing the changes in subject and verb forms across Pss 74–75. The second person singular, referring to God, dominated Ps 74 and the content was carried by lament, appeal, imperative, and questioning. Ps 75, in contrast, hosts a variety of speakers. It opens with the community's

---

42. Weiss, *Bible from Within*, 285–90.

praise of God's wondrous deeds in first person plural. God, or a spokesperson for God, is the apparent subject in vv. 2–5 who speaks in the first person singular. Verses 6–8 appear to be a commentary as third person singular subjects make declarative statements. The conclusion to the psalm (vv. 9–10) embraces two first person singular statements. Verse 9 is a praise statement, forming an *inclusio* with the first person plural praise of v. 1. Verse 10 ends the psalm with a declarative statement in the first person future tense forecasting the fates of the righteous and the wicked. God appears to be the speaker.

How can we account for the placement of this psalm of confident praise after two that provoke such crisis? Attention to shared motifs between the three psalms and the internal dynamic of Ps 75 suggest an answer.

The Experience of Devastation

The devastation described in painful detail in Ps 74 is acknowledged in Ps 75:3. People and earth "totter" (נמגים—nifal of מוג Heb 75:4). This verse echoes other descriptions in the Old Testament of the experience of overwhelming chaos. For example, Ps 46:7 (Heb.) pairs together the verbs מוט and מוג in describing the tottering of kingdoms and melting of earth.[43] Psalm 75:3 emphasizes the swaying of earth's foundations, which is part of the same creation mythology used in Ps 74:12–17.[44] First Samuel 2:8 proclaims, "for the pillars of the earth are the Lord's and on them has he set the world." Psalm 104:5 hymns the creator, "Thou didst set the earth on its foundations, so that it should never be shaken (תמוג)."

The close connection of temple with earth through the temple's containing the symbols that communicate the mythology of the creation of an orderly world permits us to see that the temple's destruction (Ps 74) would cause an experience of tottering of creation and inhabitants (Ps 75).[45] Again, this universal tottering sets the individual's slipping and stumbling in Ps 73

---

43. Some texts such as Ps 46:6, Job 9:6, and Amos 8:8 refer to God "who shakes the earth out of its place, and its pillars tremble," but others such as Ps 82:5 state that the false gods by their ignorance shake the foundations of the earth. In Isa 24:16–19 the wicked by their actions bring upon the earth a collapse similar to that of Noah's flood. While Ps 75:3 does not explicitly name the origin of the eruption, it may be the destruction of the cosmic and social order by the wicked, though the charges leveled at God in Ps 74:11 make it possible to read God as ultimately responsible.

44. See Keel, *Symbolism of the Biblical World*, 175–76.

45. Thus Samson's pulling down the pillars of the temple of Dagon is a final act of defiance of the world of the Philistines (Judg 16:23–31).

Psalms 73–75

in the widest context.⁴⁶ Thus the experience of those shamed at the hands of the wicked is actually a reflex of an upheaval of cosmic proportions.

The Divine Commitment to Save

The acknowledgment of devastation is answered by God's decision to save. Ps 75 marks a radical turn away from the state of crisis of Pss 73–74. God insists upon upholding the creation language on which world order rests, "When the earth totters, and all its inhabitants, it is I who keep steady its pillars" (75:3). God's insistence upon asserting divine claim and care over the world echoes a similar speech of divine passion to save in Exod 3:7–8: "I have observed the misery of my people who are in Egypt; I have heard their cry on account of their taskmasters. Indeed, I know their sufferings, and I have come down to deliver them from the Egyptians, and to bring them up out of that land to a good and broad land."

"It is I" indicates the restoration of the presence of God that had been the intention of the strong imperatives and interrogatives of Ps 74.⁴⁷ In this declaration to save, God answers in Ps 75 several issues that generate the complaints in Pss 73 and 74.

The Motif of the Hand of God

A study of the verb תכן (Heb. v. 3), "to keep steady," suggests that in the declaration "it is I who keep its pillars steady" the motif of the hand of God prominent in Pss 73 and 74 reappears. תכן is used in the piel to describe meting out an apportionment (Job 28:25; Isa 40:12) and in the pual to mean the counting out of money (2 Kgs 12:12), both activities that could use the hands. The motif of the hand of God becomes an illustration of the course of the spiritual experience from orientation through disorientation to reorientation that Brueggemann identified as binding the unity of the Psalter. It is instructive to display the progression of texts.

---

46. Notice in this regard the dialectic of destruction set up between individuals (Ps 73), sanctuary (Ps 74) and cosmos (Ps 75).

47. Lindstrom, *Suffering and Sin*, 97.

The Self-Shaming God Who Reconciles

Ps 73:22–23	Ps 74:11	Ps 75:3, 7–8
I was stupid and ignorant; I was like a brute beast toward you. Nevertheless, I am continually with you; you hold my right hand.	Why do you hold back your hand in your bosom?	When the earth totters with all its inhabitants, it is I who keep its pillars steady. But it is God who executes judgment; putting down one and lifting up another. For in the hand of the Lord there is a cup with foaming wine

The hand that had kept the psalmist's feet from slipping (73:2) by holding the speaker's right hand (73:23), then was withdrawn (74:11) to great dismay (74:19), now embraces the pillars of the earth (75:3) to keep steady the tottering world and its inhabitants.[48] This motif of the hand returns in 75:7–8, lifting up the downtrodden and, bearing a cup of foaming wine, judging the wicked.

God's Reply to the Boastful

If Ps 75:4–5 is now read in the light of Ps 74, it appears that God is making a reply directly to a boastful, insolent, over-confident enemy that Ps 74 describes in vv. 10, 18, 23 and Ps 73 describes in vv. 4–12 (especially vv. 8–9).[49]

Reading back through the three psalms one sees this dynamic clearly.

Ps 75:4–5	Ps 74:10, 23	Ps 73:8–9
I say to the boastful, "Do not boast," and to the wicked, "Do not lift up your horn; Do not lift up your horn on high, or speak with insolent neck."	How long, O God, is the foe to scoff / the enemy to revile your name? Similarly, v. 18. Do not forget the clamor of your foes, the uproar of your adversaries	They scoff and speak with malice; loftily they threaten oppression. They set their mouths against heaven; and their tongues range over the earth.

---

48. See 1 Sam 2:8; Job 38:4; Pss 24:2; 11:4; 82:5; 46:6. Hossfeld and Zenger, *Psalms 2*, 234, display iconography of the divinity leading the worshipper by the right hand.

49. The rare verb הלל IV, "betray," derived from הלל III, "deride, taunt," used in Ps 75:4, occurs only in Pss 5:6 and 73:3. In both places it characterizes the evildoers and wicked. See the similar characterization of the wicked in Ps 73:8–9. The identification of the wicked by the lamenter in Ps 73 is answered by divine speech in Ps 75.

The Fixing of a Time

Ps 75:2 begins "At the set time which I appoint," which now answers the plea of Ps 74:10 "How long, O God, is the foe to scoff?"

God as the Judge

Even though nothing in Ps 75 specifically identifies God as the speaker in vv. 2–5, its linkage with the crisis of Ps 74 makes this identification almost certain. In Ps 74:22 the community adopts the language of the law-court to implore God to "arise and plead thy cause." Psalm 74 calls upon God "to remember" four times (vv. 2 twice, 18 and 22) and "to not forget" twice (vv. 19 and 23).[50] The language of 75:2 promises "I will judge with equity." This promise of equitable justice is present throughout the Asaph collection. Other Asaph psalms show God judging both Israel and the nations (76:7–9; 79–83). However, the placement of Ps 75 as a definite answer to the laments of Pss 73 and 74 makes it unique in the collection in that the impact of God's judging the wicked is the salvation of Israel.[51]

The Shaming of the Wicked

The staggering of the wicked described in Ps 73:18 "Truly you set them in slippery places; you make them fall to ruin" finds its cause in God's punishment through drinking to the dregs the cup of foaming wine (Ps 75:8).[52] The contrast is clear. At the beginning of Ps 73 the speaker's feet "had almost [but not quite] stumbled, my steps had nearly slipped." In Ps 75, through the ritual of drinking the cup of punishment, God transfers to the wicked the shame that had come over the oppressed by what they experienced as God's disloyal lack of protection.[53] The verdict of Ps 1, "the

---

50. Mitchell, *Message of the Psalter*, 97–98, shows this motif to be characteristic of Asaph psalms.

51. Mitchell misses this important distinction in his attempt to portray the Asaph psalms as speaking God's judgment and play them off against the Psalms of Ascent, which emphasize God's blessing. See ibid., 171–78.

52. See similar imagery in Jer 25:15ff.; 49:12; 51:39; Isa 51:17ff.; and Ezek 23:31ff. This correspondence with exilic and post-exilic prophecy suggests to Joachim Begrich an exilic date for this psalm. See Gunkel and Begrich, *Introduction to Psalms*, 291. The imagery is best understood against the background of a banquet scene rather than trial by ordeal. See Carroll, *Jeremiah*, 502, contra McKane, "Poison, Trial by Ordeal and the Cup of Wrath," 474–92.

53. Childs is sensitive to this transfer of shame through drinking the cup of wrath in Isa 51:17–23. See his *Isaiah*, 405.

wicked shall not stand in the judgment" is confirmed again through the ritual of the foaming wine.

The Community's Praise to God

Psalm 75 contains within it an oracle of salvation (vv.2–5) spoken by God or by a prophet in God's name,[54] directed specifically to the crisis of the identity of the speaker(s) of Pss 73 and 74 that has been provoked by the collapse of God's saving presence within the temple. The community receives this oracle and identifies God as the executor of judgment (75:7). Thus the community that had once implored God not to "let the downtrodden be put to shame, but to let the poor and needy praise your name" (Ps 74:21) now praises the name of the God of Jacob who comes to lift up the downtrodden and to set things right (75:1, 7, 9–10).[55]

This divine answer to a communal plea for help followed by praise is also the pattern of the action of the Asaphite prophet responding to a national crisis in 2 Chr 20:5–17.[56] While this is a prose setting, the sequencing of a communal plea for help, recounting of past acts of salvation, and prophetic oracle of salvation followed by praise tracks closely the progress of Pss 73–75.[57] It is intriguing to ask whether this story provided the model for the bringing together of these three psalms, or whether the group of three psalms provided the "text" for the preacher. The similarity between the prophetic oracle in Chronicles and our set of three psalms uncovers yet

---

54. Mitchell, *Message of the Psalter*, 92–93, describes how the Asaphites were a temple ministry of prophetic song. The occurrences of divine oracles in Asaph Psalms are three times greater than in the rest of the Psalter. In Ps 12:5 God is clearly identified as the speaker of the oracle of salvation. The context of Ps 75 is persuasive in making this identification. Hossfeld and Zenger, *Psalms 2*, 253–54, acknowledge that the "elevated speaker" is either a speaker to the nations (though not cult prophet) or Yahweh. They opt for the elevated speaker whose words merge with God.

55. Praise does not appear frequently in the Asaph collection, and where it does praise or prayer is promised upon the occurrence of God's action. Only in Ps 75 is praise given without condition. See Gunkel and Begrich, *Introduction to Psalms*, 254.

56. Williamson, "Reading the Lament Psalms Backwards," 6. Goulder, *The Psalms of Asaph and the Pentateuch*, 316: "It has sometimes been thought rather a comedown for the great prophetic tradition to be invested in a choirman; but it is not always noticed that the prophetic movement finds voice already in our Asaph psalms . . . In Psalms 50, 81, and 82 (and perhaps 75), the Asaph psalmist thinks fit to put considerable speeches into the mouth of God . . . The Asaphites knew that they were heirs to a prophetic ministry from Bethel days."

57. Gunkel and Begrich, *Introduction to Psalms*, 265, calls Ps 75 a "prophetic liturgy."

another linkage between Pss 74 and 75. The lament of 74:9 "We do not see our signs; there is no longer any prophet, and there is none among us who knows how long?" is now answered by the prophetic oracle of salvation in 75:2–5. In essence God becomes God's own prophet.[58]

The conversation among Pss 73, 74, and 75 produces a powerful statement of the saving God of Israel whose presence experienced afresh turns back the shame of God's people upon the arrogant. The remaining verses of Ps 75 add specificity to this conclusion.

When we turn to the commentary, Ps 75:6 (Eng.; Heb. v. 7), the speaker makes clear that the help promised in the oracle of salvation will be from God alone:[59] "For neither from the east nor from the west, neither from the desert [south] nor from the mountains [north]"—the four cardinal points on the compass.[60] This concentration upon God's intervention as exclusive savior reaches its fullest expression in Books IV and V of the Psalter.

The conclusion of the psalm (vv. 9 and 10) contains three statements in first person singular. In v. 9 the speaker twice praises God for acts of judging the wicked and restoring the downtrodden. This verse forms an *inclusio* with the line of praise that opens the psalm. The praise that begins and ends Ps 75 anticipates those psalms that praise God's sole kingship in Book V.

The third first-person singular statement occurs in v. 10, which functions like an answer to this praise: "All the horns of the wicked I will cut off, but the horns of the righteous shall be exalted." While the speaker is not identified, taken in context with the challenge to the boastful in vv. 4 and 5 "Do not lift up your horn," it surely must be God. As if in answer to human praise, God forecasts the fates of the righteous and the wicked when God sets matters to right in the future. The language is a strong echo of the ending of Ps 1, "for the Lord knows the way of the righteous, but the way of the wicked will perish." The crisis of shame that confronted the speaker of Ps 73, made unbearable by the destruction of the temple in Ps 74, was that the speaker could no longer count on God to know the way of the righteous. Thus the oracle of salvation pronounced in Ps 75:3 "when the earth totters . . . it is I who keep its pillars steady," now reiterated in verse

---

58. Roberts, "Of Signs, Prophets, and Time Limits," 474–81.

59. See the similar emphasis in 2 Chr 20:17, "This battle is not for you to fight . . . see the victory of the Lord on your behalf."

60. So NAB and JB (Eng. v. 6) following LXX, reading הרים (Heb. v. 7) not as an infinitive construct of רום.

10, acts to reaffirm the claims of divine faithfulness in Pss 1 and 2, which, with the collapse of the monarchy, had provoked theological shame.[61] Even though the time of reaffirmation is lodged in a future redemptive act of God, the community's immediate praise indicates that faith and identity have been restored.[62]

In sum, Pss 73–75 appear to have been placed carefully at the center of the Psalter to sound the notes that will become the dominant chords of the bulk of Books III–V. These three psalms are a microcosm that illustrates what is yet to be read in the Psalter.[63] As the traditional institutions under girding Israel's identity give way, the community looks solely to God for restoration and praises God alone as king.[64] While each psalm can be studied as a closed poem, they resound with greater depth and intensity as they speak to each other and together. Within this larger context, themes are modified and enriched by intense interaction with other themes. By a complex system of cross-referencing, the message of God's act to confirm fidelity in the face of shame receives a fresh and compelling hearing.[65]

THE ESCHATOLOGICAL TRAJECTORY OF PSALM 75

The witness of God's insistent affirmation to save, spoken in the midst of disappointed trust in God and consequence shame of God-fearers, becomes fertile ground for the nurturing of eschatological hope in the lives of those who read the Psalms of any generation. Susan Gillingham has recently demonstrated how the final shapers of the Psalter and the translators of the Septuagint have set an eschatological/prophetic bias on the Psalms.

---

61. The foundation for God's being faithful to the two-ways formula lies in God's own revealing of divine character in Exod 34:6 as bipolar attributes of justice and mercy. We develop this theme in chapter 3.

62. Gunkel and Begrich, *Introduction to the Psalms*, 274.

63. Wilson, *The Editing of the Hebrew Psalter*, 215, declares Book IV to be "the 'editorial center' of the final form of the Hebrew Psalter."

64. Psalm 76 extends the hymn of praise of Ps 75. Hossfeld and Zenger, *Psalms 2*, puts 73–75 in a compositional arc of Teaching-Lament-Oracle/God's Response (comprising 75 and 76). The attempt of Jensen, "Psalm 75: Its Poetic Context and Structure," 416–29, to link Pss 74–76 through showing how each psalm corresponds to a section of Ps 73 fails in my judgment. While emphasizing the crucial position and role of Ps 73, his approach interrupts the integrity of each psalm, which is key to appreciating their complex relationships. Jensen attempts to describe a liturgical function of these psalms rather than to relate them canonically.

65. For a comparable model in New Testament interpretation, see Tannehill, "The Magnificat as Poem," 263–75.

The royal psalms now are read in anticipation of a renewed kingship in some future time. But Ps 75 in the LXX receives a direct eschatological stamp through the translation of part of its superscript למנצח. Gillingham explains: "Although this could be read as a piel participle of נצח ('one who excels,' or 'one who is preeminent') such as a leader of worship, as in 1 Chr 15:21, another reading, taking מנצח as a substantive of נצח could simply mean 'for eternity.' This interpretation seems to have been intended by the LXX translators, rendering למנצח as εἰς τὸ τέλος, which could be interpreted as 'for eternity' (i.e., for the end of time, or for the last things)."[66]

This eschatological stamp made the Psalter particularly attractive to the New Testament church as it searched the Scriptures for understanding Jesus as the inbreaking of the end of time through the eschatological acts of his death and resurrection. The broad themes of these three psalms find a compelling reappearance in the New Testament witness to Jesus' crucifixion and to the preaching of the resurrection. In chapter 4, we will situate the witness of Pss 73–75 within the Christian canon and offer a constructive statement within the context of Trinitarian theology.

---

66 Gillingham, "From Liturgy to Prophecy," 479.

2

To Be Shamed, Living beyond Shame

Listening to the witness of Pss 73–75 has uncovered an important issue of theological and pastoral significance—the issue of theological shame. It is now appropriate to give a systematic accounting of this topic. This will contribute to framing the suggestions for pastoral leadership with believers and congregations in living beyond shame.

The shame experienced through a betrayal of trust, the suffering of a failed risk, can give rise to a variety of affections, such as anger, disgust, or a feeling of being violated. Stories from 1–2 Samuel offer examples of the shame caused by broken trust.

David speaks in anger over his shame of suffering a failed risk when he perceives how Nabal has not kept faith with him. "Surely in vain have I guarded all that this fellow has in the wilderness . . . and he has returned me evil for good" (1 Sam 25:21).[1] Nabal's refusal to reward David and his men for "protecting" his flock is, in the words of Nabal's wife, Abigail, a betrayal of trust (נבלה), a word that denotes an offence to the deep structure of society (1 Sam 25:25),[2] and David himself characterizes this refusal as an insult

---

1. Stansell, "Honor and Shame," 101–5. He also points to the roots of the confrontation between Saul and Jonathan (1 Sam 20:30–34) as Saul's perception that by Jonathan's protecting David, Jonathan has broken faith with his father and brought shame upon Saul.

2. נבלה is "a general expression for serious disorderly and unruly action resulting in the breakup of an existing relationship whether between tribes, within the family, in a business arrangement, in marriage or with God. It indicates the end of an existing order consequent upon breach of rules that maintained that order. In other words נבלה refers to a violation of the sacred taboos that define, hedge, and protect the structure of society. It is a sacrilege." McCarter, Jr., *II Samuel,* 322–23. See also Keefe, "Rapes of Women/Wars of Men," 82. The castigating of oneself as "foolish" (סכל; niphal) in confessions of breaking trust occurs in 1 Sam 26:21 where Saul contrasts his murderous pursuit of the fugitive

(נבלה 1 Sam 25:39). Of course, the name Nabal itself is a hypostatization of נבל (fool; 1 Sam 25:25).

נבלה, חרקה, נבל reoccur in the story of the rape of Tamar by her half-brother Amnon (2 Samuel 13).[3] Tamar pleads with Amnon at the point of his raping her, "Don't, my brother! Don't force me. Such a thing should not be done in Israel! Don't do this wicked thing (נבלה). What about me? Where could I get rid of my disgrace/insult (חרקה)? And what about you? You would be like one of the wicked fools (נבלים) in Israel" (2 Sam 13:13–14). This tightly crafted speech captures key words that describe the axis of trust-betrayal-shame.[4] Tamar's speech is reasoning and law-referencing. She is trying to protect her brother from consequences of wanton folly and herself from the inability to bear insult. She upholds and calls to mind community standards, and social structure. Tamar references the framework of life in which she lives, takes refuge, and in which she puts her trust.

The Joseph narrative includes a story where similar issues of trust and the betrayal of trust are at stake.[5] In Genesis 39 Potiphar entrusts everything into the hands of the servant, Joseph, except his wife (vv. 2–6a). She repeatedly confronts him with the command, "Lie with me," the very words Amnon directed to his sister. Like Tamar, Joseph parries her advances with speech that makes clear that to accede to the command to have sex with Potiphar's wife would break trust with Potiphar and put him to shame[6] (vv. 8–9). When Joseph flees her most blatant advance, she, in her cover-up,

---

David with David's sparing Saul's life out of loyalty to the king. The same verb in the hiphil is used to describe David's hubris in taking the census of soldiers in 2 Sam 24:10.

3. Trible, *Texts of Terror,* and Keefe, "Rapes of Women/Wars of Men," 91–92. For a treatment of Tamar's rape that prefigures God's abandonment of Israel to exile see Gray, "Amnon: A Chip off the Old Block?" 39–54. In this exposition, the focus is shifted from wisdom traditions to prophetic critique of the monarchy. Tamar is not viewed primarily as a victim of foolishness but as a tool in the struggle for succession. Freedman analyzes this story's literary features. The rape of Tamar is the concluding frame to the "super J" narrative that begins with a similar story of the rape of Dinah by Shechem. Freedman, "Dinah and Shechem, Tamar and Amnon," 51–63.

4. Marsh, "Amnon's Folly," 141–43, and Camp, "The Wise Women of 2 Samuel," 14–29. The comparison of Tamar's story with that of the wise woman, Abigail, is interesting in how these speeches are responded to in opposite ways. David (1 Sam 25:32–34) heeds Abigail, while Amnon refused to listen to Tamar (2 Sam 13:14, 16). See the admonition to listen to wise counsel in Prov 12:15; 19:20.

5. Alter, *The David Story,* 267–68.

6. See Westermann, *Joseph, Eleven Bible Studies on Genesis,* 25.

accuses him of attempted rape and charges this as an insult to Potiphar's trust.

Even though the two rape attempts have opposite outcomes, they share in common the devastation that betrayal of trust leaves in its wake.[7] The description of the raped and evicted Tamar as "a ruin" (שממה 2 Sam 13:20)[8] and the casting of Joseph into prison point to a bleak future for both as inferior people.

The devastation from broken trust is amply illustrated in the story of Abaslom's rebellion. David, in his grief for his slain son Absalom, does not acknowledge the risks undertaken by his army that fought successfully to save his throne. Joab must point out to him how he "has covered with shame the faces of all your servants, who have this day saved your life . . . because you love those who hate you and hate those who love you. You have made it clear today that commanders and officers are nothing to you" (2 Sam 19:5–7).[9] David's acting as if his commanders and servants are "nothing to you" illustrates what it means to shame another person. Indeed, the parallel phrases "shall be ashamed/shall be as nothing" in

---

7. Cooper-White begins her book *The Cry of Tamar* with an eclectic exegesis of the rape of Tamar. "I do not come to this exegesis with the methodological purity of a scholar using only a social-culture, literary, rhetorical, or linguistic lens for analysis. Rather, I come as a hungry and passionate preacher and pastor, to glean whatever meanings I can about Tamar's shadowed history from whatever approaches seem to shed more light" (5). She highlights what to her are the patriarchal biases of the narrator and imports into Tamar the trauma of rape that she sees missing in the text. She does not deal with the shame-insult-fool issues in the context of the betrayal of social structure. She sees this story raising issues of justice that damn the early monarchy. Cooper-White does, however, raise the question for Tamar that is implicit in the theology of the succession narrative, the providence of God in securing the successor to David: Where is God's providence for Tamar? This is the question that a theology of shared shame addresses.

8. "'Send this away' (v.17), Amnon is speaking not to but about the woman who stands in his presence. She has become for him solely a disposable object . . . The Hebrew has only the demonstrative *this*. For Amnon, Tamar is a thing, a 'this' he wants thrown out. She is trash" (Tribble, *Texts of Terror*, 48). Moffatt's paraphrase, "Put out this wench," highlights Tamar's damaged sense of self caused by Amnon's putting her to shame (*The Moffatt Translation of the Bible*, 361).

9. Olyan, "Honor, Shame, and Covenant Relations," 208–11, describes David's action as failing to "act appropriately toward his loyal servants" with the result that "the legitimate covenant expectations of a victorious army were not met . . . Thus David's act constituted a covenant violation. David has apparently gone beyond his rights as suzerain and broken covenant."

Isa 41:11 confirm this interpretation as well as similar parings in Jer 12:13 and 1 Cor 1:27–28.[10]

Turning to the Psalter, a striking example of the trauma of the shame of betrayal occurs in Ps 55.[11] The psalmist describes explicitly the emotive force of this shame.

> My heart is in anguish within me,
>   the terrors of death have fallen upon me.
> Fear and trembling come upon me,
>   and horror overwhelms me. (vv. 4–5)

The catalyst for such trauma lies in the underlying betrayal of a friend.

> My companion laid hands on a friend
>   and violated a covenant with me.
> With speech smoother than butter,
>   but with a heart set on war;
> with words that were softer than oil
>   but in fact were drawn swords. (vv. 20–21)

Moving from the arena of human relations, what we are identifying as theological shame happens when someone who has placed trust in God is caught in events that compel the belief that God has betrayed this trust. An expression of theological shame that closely parallels David's experience of Nabal's ingratitude is found in the Servant's negative evaluation of the outcome of the call God gave him: "I have labored in vain, I have spent my strength for nothing and vanity" (Isa 49:4).[12]

In Pss 73–75 we listen to humans suffering from perceiving that a risk of trust in God has failed. By calling this experience of betrayal "theological shame" we are pointing to how believers are making sense out of their crisis. It is helpful to be reminded of Margaret Odell's observation:

> In [the complaint] Psalms, the plea not to be put to shame is often combined with the Psalmist's confession that he has put his trust in God (Pss 25:2, 20; 31:2). The plea, "I have trusted in you; let me not be put to shame," appeals to God to honor the petitioner's dependence. If the Psalmist should experience distress, sickness or the scorn of his community, then that is because God has failed

---

10. Stansell, "Honor and Shame," 109–11.

11. Ramsay, "Confronting Family Violence and its Spiritual Damage," 28–40. The theme of "intimate enemies" has been explored by Sheppard in "'Enemies' and the Politics of Prayer in the Book of Psalms," 61–82.

12. Compare Elijah's complaint in 1 Kgs 19:14.

him . . . It is also worth noting that the expression of shame is the opposite of what we would consider the feeling of unworthiness; rather, it is the expression of an individual's outrage [protest] that others do not acknowledge and respond to his or her claims."[13]

Elsewhere in the Psalter, Ps 44:8–9 contrasts shame with boasting as basic experiences of Israel's relationship with God: "In God we have boasted continually, and we will give thanks to your name forever. Yet you have rejected us and abased us, and have not gone out with our armies." Confidence and shame frame the contours of the speaker's life before God. They inform and structure the strong entreaty for God to wake up and redeem God's people.

The pathos of the betrayal of trusted relationships is reflected in God's own pathos when meeting the unanticipated betrayal by God's people. While a full exploration of this theme lies outside the scope of this book, attention should be paid to the way Israel's prophets picture God reacting to Israel's disobedience as the betrayal of an anticipated response.[14]

Isaiah pictures Israel as a vineyard (5:1–7). God planted it with choice vines, expecting a good crop, but God was disappointed because bitter grapes are the unanticipated result.[15]

> What more was there to do for my vineyard
>   that I have not done in it?
> When I expected it to yield grapes,
>   why did it yield wild grapes?

The song suggests that appearances can be deceiving, that grapes that looked good turned out to be bitter. This suggestion is strengthened by the punning that occurs in the final words of indictment.

---

13. See fn. 19, chapter 1.

14. See the classic statement of this theme in Heschel, *The Prophets*. For a discussion from the perspective of Reformed theology of several issues associated with God's vulnerability to human activity, see Rigby, "Providence and Play," 10–18.

15. For critical issues in interpretation, Childs, *Isaiah*, 41–46. Shiryon comments helpfully on the communication tactics of detachment and emotional involvement employed in this song of the vineyard in "Biblical Roots of Literatherapy," 8–9. Williams, "Frustrated Expectations in Isaiah V 1–7," 459–65, attends to the theme of multiple interpretative frustrations in the song that enable the reader to identify with God's frustration, but Carr, *The Erotic Word*, 59–90, sees this text projecting male jealousy over a female considered as a possession. He does not give attention to the bewilderment and shame of the vineyard owner over the vines not acting according to nature, with the accompanying mystery of sinister infection of the vines, requiring dismantling of the vineyard.

[God] expected justice (מִשְׁפָּט),
    but saw bloodshed (מִשְׂפָּח);
righteousness (צְדָקָה),
    but heard a cry (צְעָקָה)!

God's bewilderment and anger issue out of a sense profound disappointment over this unnatural response in God's people who pretended to make good on the trusted result.

And now I will tell you
what I will do to my vineyard.
I will . . . make it a waste

Hosea pictures Israel as the incorrigible son who matches God's long-suffering care with deepening rejection (11:1–11). Israel was totally focused on turning away from any behavior God had placed trust in God's children to evidence. Again, God's anger at Israel issues from this sense of bewilderment and sorrow over Israel's acting against what was covenantally expected and underscores the reality of the sense of betrayal felt in God.[16]

Jeremiah radically exposes Israel's unnatural rebellion through the shocking symbolic action of the loincloth (13:1–11). Jeremiah's wearing this item of personal apparel symbolized God's commitment to the intimate nature of the relationship between God and Israel/Judah. This action also communicated to Jeremiah the depth of God's closeness to God's people. The people were to cling to God as a loincloth clings to a man. As a loincloth makes a man so the people were to do for God—exist as God's possession, a name, a praise and a glory.[17] The removal of the loincloth, its burial in the muddy river bank, and subsequent retrieval—all by divine command—exposed how it was "good for nothing," demonstrating how even with God's making Israel cling to God like a loincloth, "they would not listen" and are good for nothing. Again, the expected result did not rub off on the people, and God's decision to destroy disobedient Israel testifies to the anger of being betrayed.[18]

---

16. Wolff, *Hosea*, 193, 201.

17. The preaching of Deut 10:12–21 provides a commentary on this symbolic action. The two texts share key words רבק (cling, Deut 10:20; Jer 13:11) and תהלה (praise, Deut 10:21; Jer 13:11) and themes of a chosen people for whose sake God has manifested God's glory as well as an exhortation to keep faith with God. Miller, "The Psalms as a Mediation on the First Commandment," 96. The relationship between Jeremiah and Deuteronomy has been extensively studied.

18. Heschel, *The Prophets*, 117; Brueggemann, *A Commentary on Jeremiah*, 126–29.

Even this limited probe into the human frustration of divine expectations indicates both the subtlety of the theme of betrayal of entrusted behavior in the Bible and the complex of affections and actions such betrayal evokes. A common theme emerges of the acting against expected results (rotten grapes/incorrigible son/unsupportive loincloth) with the accompanying lament of God: Why? This theme is grounded in "an ineffably transcendent God who yet communicates dynamically with the created world and is self-exposed to the wounds and limitations of reciprocity with the elect people and with all humanity."[19] In chapter 4 I will show how the biblical demonstration of both human and divine disappointment, bewilderment and double-cross, which the Old Testament groups under the category shame, will be transformed by the New Testament witness to the self-shaming God.

DIVINE CLAIMS, HUMAN THREAT, DIVINE RESOLUTION

Returning to Pss 73–75, theological shame makes its first appearance in Ps 73 with the speaker's expostulation, "All in vain have I kept my hands clean" (v.13) This experience of theological shame intensifies in Ps 74 with the destruction of the holy place as the defeated cry, "Have regard for thy covenant . . . Let not the downtrodden be put to shame" (vv. 20–21).

Clearly, speakers of such expressions are posing critical questions to such fundamentals as God's promises of faithfulness to God's people and God's capability of remaining true to these promises. It is important to note that the speaker confesses to nothing that would have caused this situation, and that this position is not challenged. Our investigation of theological shame and its resolution reveals a powerful dynamic at work throughout the Psalter to uphold God's fidelity when God is confronted with critical questioning of this fidelity.

Origen (185–253) was one of the earliest interpreters of this text to sense God's dependence upon humans rendering faithfulness. He makes the bold assertion that the loincloth describes the people acting "like a shelter for God" against heresy. Ledegang, "Images of the Church in Origen: the Girdle (Jeremiah 13,1–11)," 908.

19. Lewis, *Between Cross and Resurrection*, 113. The lament of God has been structured liturgically in the "Reproaches" a series of alternating versicles and responses that are sung on Good Friday. Each reproach begins "O my people, what have I done to you? In what have I wearied you? Answer me," which is taken from Mic 6:3. Each reproach alternates between summaries of faithful acts of God and the betrayal of that faithfulness in the events of Good Friday, culminating in a plea for mercy. Cross and Livingstone, *The Oxford Dictionary of the Christian Church*, 1175.

This dynamic is generated to protect the claims of torah-piety since these claims provide the base line for understanding the rise of theological shame. The deliberate placement of Ps 1 as the interpretative prism for hearing the Psalter pushes to the forefront the linkage of the fulfillment of God's promises with obedience to "torah" in its broadest meaning as instruction. Pss 19 and 119 remind readers of the importance of the claims of torah-piety. These claims are summarized repeatedly in the psalms through the formula of the "two ways." The classical expression of this formula is in Ps 1, "For the Lord knows the way of the righteous, but the way of the wicked will perish."[20] This formula rests on divine authority.

While walking in either of the two ways is attended by actual consequences, the primary emphasis is on experiencing a quality of relationship. "The Lord *knows* the way of the righteous." Indeed Ps 139 links the Lord's knowing with the most intimate depths of the subconscious. Psalm 37:18–20 repeats and expands the two-ways formula, combining the Lord's knowing the blameless and their not being put to shame in evil times.

> The Lord knows the days of the blameless,
>   and their heritage will abide forever;
> they are not put to shame in evil times,
>   in the days of famine they have abundance.

This statement is a confession of trust, a position upon which the believer risks a stance in the midst of contradictory evidence.

The statement of the claim of torah-piety in Ps 1 is augmented by Ps 2 in a similar claim of divine choice of David as God's son and subsequent bequeathing of world hegemony to the Davidic lineage. These claims are reiterated in Ps 72. Thus torah-piety and faithfulness to David's house, taken together, become a multifaceted prism through which the life of the believer in the Psalter is to be understood.

When the believer experiences a quality of life that denies the efficacy of this arrangement, the believer concludes that God in whom he or she has put their trust has proven false.[21] It is here that theological shame erupts

---

20. See fn. 29, chapter 1.

21. Sölle in her searching examination of suffering describes this link between that experience and Godforsakenness. "All extreme suffering evokes the experience of being forsaken by God. In the depth of suffering people see themselves as abandoned and forsaken by everyone. That which gave life its meaning has become empty and void: it turned out to be an error, an illusion that is shattered, a guilt that cannot be rectified, a void." *Suffering*, 85. Hossfeld and Zenger, *Psalms 2*, 225–26, point to intellectual and religious suffering based on previous views of life and of the world; "a suffering because

The Self-Shaming God Who Reconciles

with enough force to shake the very foundations upon which the believer's world rests. We can trace this thread of shame through Pss 73–75.

Psalm 73 confronts the breakdown of the confident promises of Ps 1 that "the Lord knows the way of the righteous, but the way of the wicked shall perish."[22] While Ps 1:3 maintains of the righteous, "In all that he does, he prospers," the speaker of Ps 73 admits to disorienting envy "when I saw the prosperity of the wicked" (v. 3). The failure of "delight in the law" to bring for the Psalmist prosperity "in all that they do" (Ps 1:2–3) coupled with seeing exploiters enjoying ill-gotten prosperity while mocking God's impotence makes the speaker cry, "All in vain have I kept my heart pure and washed my hands in innocence" (v. 13).

Though the feeling of shame is resolved by the end of the psalm with a tensive reaffirmation of the "two ways" formula, this is quickly demolished with the emotional upheaval of Ps 74 that attends the destruction of the sanctuary: "Have regard for your covenant . . . Do not let the downtrodden be put to shame" (vv. 20–21). Here the threat to the claims of the Davidic covenant amplifies the threatened claims of torah-piety in Ps 1.

The crisis of Ps 74 flows unresolved into Ps 75. Ps 75 registers the magnitude of this double threat through the seismic description of the tottering of the earth's pillars. God responds to this threat by acts reiterating a divine commitment to save the shamed one and judge the perpetrators. Significantly, this psalm concludes with a ringing affirmation of the two-ways formula (e.g., Pss 1, 19, and 119). Clearly, the great pains taken to confront and meet the threat of theological shame are a measure of the importance attached to reaffirming torah-piety and its continuing efficacy.

Re-tracing quickly the thread of theological shame through Pss 73–75, reveals how theological shame becomes a major threat to the foundations of torah-piety and Davidic rule, calling forth a vigorous defense of God's fidelity. Consequently, God refreshes the commitment of the shamed believer to move beyond shame to life abundant securely within the boundaries of the promises and expectations of God.

---

of the speaker's ideas of God, indeed, because of God. Here is a fundamental god-crisis, resulting in structural suffering, namely the refutation of the good and just, saving and happiness-giving God by social and political realities."

22. Brueggemann, "The Cunning Little Secret of Certitude," 63–80.

THE MODALITIES OF ENGAGEMENT
WITH THEOLOGICAL SHAME

In our study of Pss 73–75, the experience of theological shame comes to verbal expression principally through two avenues. First, in Ps 73 the speaker is looking retrospectively over a passage from shame to a tensive resolution, and the language is descriptive, reflective, introspective, and contemplative.[23] Indeed, the affinity of Ps 73 to certain types of wisdom literature has been noticed.[24] Second, in Ps 74, the shame-causing events have no resolution. The unrelieved burden of shame is carried by the lament, and here the language is intrusive, intense, insistent, impatient, and imperative.[25] The juxtaposition of these contrasting modalities is instructive, for both pieces illustrate from distinct perspectives the dialectic that operates in theological shame between protesting God and yet trusting the God against whom protest is lodged.[26] As the reader reflects on how this dialectic plays itself out in these twin psalms, one gains a deepened appreciation of the depth and intensity of the engagement with theological shame in the life of faith.[27]

In Ps 73 "All in vain" is a live option. It signals a readiness to give up on the claims of torah piety and the God who stands behind them. The speaker's feet were poised to stumble and slip, taking him/her over to the side of those who scoff at God. By the speaker's own accounting, his/her soul was embittered and he/she was pricked in heart. Yet, this very person finds their way to the sanctuary of God where a new experience of God's reliability is vouchsafed.

The question becomes unavoidable: Why would one have been prompted to go to the sanctuary of God when one's experience of shame had created a lack of trust in God? The answer to this question must be

---

23. Hossfeld and Zenger, *Psalms 2*, 224, calls this psalm a 'pastorally' oriented prayer monologue that is spoken, though in the form of an explicit address to God in prayer, to human addresses, teaching, admonishing, and encouraging them.

24. See fn. 17, chapter 1.

25. Brown and Miller, *Lament*, xiii–xvi; Brueggemann, "The Formfulness of Grief," 84–97.

26. Miller provides a succinct summary of this dialectic in "Prayer as Persuasion," 356–62.

27. Brueggemann traces this engagement of Israel and God with the categories of incommensurability and mutuality in "The Psalms in Theological Use," 581–602. The mutuality between God and Israel consists of a God whose incommensurability includes a willingness to be interrupted by the unsilenceable insistence of Israel's pain and indignity.

sought in v. 15, which literary analysis has identified as the pivot point around which the psalm is perfectly balanced.[28] "If I had said, 'I will talk on in this way,' I would have been untrue to the circle of your children."

This astonishing remark testifies to the power of a faith community to exert its expectation upon the speaker.[29] The tug of the "circle of your children" still holds when trust in God proves ill founded. Against the force of shame that makes the speaker's feet slip and stumble, responsibility and obligation to those "who trust me" is more powerful. The community and its reference points set a limit to how far shame-talk can go in making sense out of the speaker's situation. Community understandings operate to make "wearisome" the speaker's understanding of his/her situation, indicating that the speaker has not yet bought into the position of the wicked.[30] The tug of the community creates a stake for it in the eventual outcome of the speaker's crisis. The community's stake looms larger than the individual's doubt. Corporate affirmations finally trump personal shame and draw the disputing speaker back into the sanctuary.

Thus, the commitment to remain true to "the circle of thy children" curbs personal speech about shame and draws one into the sanctuary where God vouchsafes a revelation of nearness.[31] But for the hold of "the circle of thy children" upon the Psalmist this revelation might not have occurred.[32]

---

28. See chapter 1, n. 23

29. This has not been recognized by the standard commentaries.

30. The wisdom tradition is keenly aware of unresolved struggle, almost to the point of giving up, to make sense out of one's experience. See Eccl 8:17 and Prov 30:2–3. In Ps 73 the fact that the wicked are not in trouble (עמל) as other mortals are (v. 5) is played off against the weariness (עמל) of the speaker (v. 16).

31. The story of barren Hanna's plea and the priest Eli's response is another instance of a lamenting person being re-oriented in the sanctuary (1 Sam 1). See Ricoeur's perceptive insight. ". . . a regained trust must finally be anchored in the recalling of what is immemorial. No doubt this is why Andre LaCocque notes that 'the lament belongs to the liturgy, that is, both to history reduced to its sacred core and its ritual actualization of the past . . . and to its prolepsis, its "preview" of the future.'" "Lamentation as Prayer," 218.

32. Psalm 69:6 approaches the relationship between the psalm-speaker and community from the opposite (speaker's) perspective.

> Let not those who hope in thee be put to shame through me . . .
> Let not those who seek thee be brought to dishonor through me.

Here the psalmist voices commitment to the preservation in the community of trust in God in persuading God not to make him/her an instance of creating distrust. I owe this insight to Riemann, "Dissonant Pieties: John Calvin," 374.

To Be Shamed, Living beyond Shame

This revelation effects a reconfiguration of theological reality that operates to reaffirm the validity of the claims of torah-piety. The conventional assumption that God assigns material goods to those who are upright, having been demolished by the prosperity of the wicked, is now replaced by the notion of goodness as defined by the nearness of God to the believer. Indeed, the speaker effects a fundamental devaluing of the power of all things physical to nurture integrity, favoring instead an intimate relationship of God.

> Whom have I in heaven but you?
> And there is nothing on earth that I desire other than you.
> My flesh and my heart may fail,
> but God is the strength of my heart and my portion forever. (v. 25)

In addition to effecting this devaluing, the passage from shame to renewed commitment to the claims of torah-piety also causes profound self-reflection and incorporation of the experience of shame resolved into a new view of the self.[33] The speaker frankly acknowledges that in the throes of the emotive force of shame (soul embittered, heart pricked v. 21) a devaluation of his/her status before God occurred (stupid, ignorant; like a brute beast toward you. v. 22).[34] Despite his/her descent into sub-human and froward behavior, the speaker confesses to have intimate knowledge of God's continued faithfulness and God's continued promise to undergird integrity into the future. This disparity of experience—retrospective negative self-evaluation coincident with a sense of divine faithfulness—the speaker integrates into his/her character through the dimension of awe: "Whom have I in heaven but you? And there is nothing on earth that I desire other than you" (v. 25).[35]

---

33. In this regard, see the insightful comments of Duff, "Recovering Lamentation," 7, and the description of "haunted truth-telling" in Jones, "Emmaus Witnessing," 121: "[W]hat are we called to be if not those who testify, who try to tell the story of what happened in its fullness; those who witness, who receive the story of violence and create a safe space for its healing; those who re-imagine the future by telling yet again—now with the event of violence woven into it—the story of our faith?"

34. Miller "Heaven's Prisoners," 17, cites an observation by Elaine Scarry (*The Body in Pain*) that pain is language shattering, causing a reversion to the pre-language of cries and groans. This insight compares with the Psalmist's description of behaving like a brute beast.

35. See Brueggemann's powerful illustration of this point in "The Third World of Evangelical Imagination," 9–27.

The Self-Shaming God Who Reconciles

Out of this awe, praise to God becomes the linguistic clue that shame has released its hold on the speaker. Indeed, praise to God is the critical indicator that one has passed from the realm of behaving as brute beast and has rejoined the ranks of those who acknowledge their creaturely status before God.[36] Significantly, the confident reaffirmation of the two-ways claim of torah-piety at the conclusion of Ps 73 ends with the personal commitment to praise, "I have made the Lord God my refuge, to tell of all your works."

As we have seen, this tensive settlement of the question of theological shame[37] collapses in Ps 74. The fundamental devaluation of physical attributes of God's goodness to the faithful in Ps 73 proves no match for coping with the devastation of the structure of the holy place. Whereas in Ps 73 the one caught in the throes of shame called himself/herself a brute beast, in Ps 74 those so shamed see their oppressors as wild animals (v. 19). Whereas in Ps 73, the tone of the speaker was wistful, envious, and self-deprecating, in Ps 74 theological shame incites rage, command, hectoring. Whereas in Ps 73, the praise of God came as response to the resolution of the shameful experience, in Ps 74:12–17 the shamed speaker praises God in something akin to a motivational lecture whose single object is to prompt out of lethargy divine intervention. One might even say that the shamed speaker is shaming God into action. Clearly, the speaker of this psalm is committed to living in the high tension between trust in God and protest to God.[38]

What might account for these large shifts is that what is at stake has grown exponentially. The holy place/sanctuary to which the tug of the community in Ps 73 had drawn the shamed believer is now destroyed. In Ps 74, the community has lost its dwelling place of God, its center and reference point, which makes impossible any reorientation of spirit out of a

---

36. See also Sölle's analysis of the conquest of powerlessness by observing the movement from being speechless to becoming aware, able to speak and ultimately to organizing, *Suffering*, 73. In *Singing for Survival*, Flam documents the artistic activity of the Jewish ghetto of Lodz, Poland, during Nazi occupation. It is a compelling description of the critical importance of speech and song for sustaining a community's sense of integrity.

37. See fn. 30, chapter 1.

38. For further development, see Balentine, *Prayer in the Hebrew Bible*. Olyan, "Honor, Shame and Covenant Relations," 206–7, cites the absence of evidence in extra-biblical literature of accusations of the suzerain of breaking covenant. For a profound exposition of the life of inevitable protest against theological shame from one whose heritage is in the Holocaust, consult Blumenthal, *Facing the Abusing God*. See also Penchansky, *What Rough Beast?*

To Be Shamed, Living beyond Shame

disorienting situation. The community has lost its defenders of the holy place, and this psalm becomes the first expression of shame over divine defaulting on the claims of Davidic protection in Ps 2. Faced with the abolition of its symbolic world of order, the blanket of theological shame threatens to suffocate the community, prompting its gut-wrenching lament. Faced with the collapse of the prism through which may be viewed the intention of God for human life, the witness of the Psalter if not all Scripture becomes profoundly suspect. Faced with the collapse of institutional supports of community, the poor, downtrodden and needy are vulnerable to violation (vv. 20–21).

Psalm 75 responds succinctly and pointedly to this amplified statement of theological shame. Clearly, God will maintain sole divine right to judge and rescue. The hand of God plays an important metaphorical role in the resolution of theological shame into renewed confidence and praise. The earth's tottering pillars, symbols of both community and individual stability, are steadied. As judge God gives a hand up to the downtrodden, and hands the wicked the cup of shame to drink.[39] The combined effect of these actions is God's guiding the community of faith in interpreting afresh the claims of torah piety and strengthening the community's role in shaping its members in conformity with these claims.

The heavy emphasis on praise, both introducing and concluding this psalm, indicates that the return of the speech of praise marks the lifting of shame. The two-ways claim of torah-piety receives a conclusive affirmation. The claim of Davidic protection does not receive similar assurance, being substituted by the promise of divine immediate initiative. As befits the canonical positioning of these psalms as the overture for the last half of the Psalter, statements of divine initiative to judge and rescue are necessarily broad and open-ended. Psalms 73–75 as overture, illustrate what is yet to be read in the Psalter. As the traditional institutions undergirding identity give way, the community looks solely to God for restoration and praises God alone as king.

---

39. Brueggemann, "A Text That Redescribes," 3–19, speaks about the failure of the dominant script of post-modern culture (amnesia to the past of generosity-despair to the future of fidelity-anxiety in the present of a never ending work of self-invention and self-sufficiency). It is intriguing to think of the cup of staggering in light of the failure of a dominant script.

3

Shame as a Theological Crisis

PSALM 73 AS COMMENTARY ON THE BOOK OF MALACHI

A striking parallel to Ps 73 is found in Malachi 3. Malachi 3:13–15 describes an encounter between God and Israel structured in the form of accusation, question and answer.[1] God begins the dialogue by accusing Israel of hurtful speech[2] when God hears, "It is vain to serve God. What do we profit by keeping his command or by going about as mourners before the Lord of hosts? Now we count the arrogant happy; evildoers not only prosper but when they put God to the test they escape." It is remarkable how God's complaint succinctly expresses the complaint of Ps 73 with parallel themes of the prosperity of evildoers, the impotence of God's judgment, and the shame of vain service to God. (vv. 4–9, 11, 13) God complains to Israel of Israel's complaint against God!

The resolution of this complaint (Mal 3:16–18) bears allusions to the dynamic of Ps 73 as well. In the psalms, communal discipline stimulated intense discernment by the shamed one in the sanctuary which yielded a reassertion of the validity of the "two ways." (v. 27–28) In Malachi, some[3] of

---

1. Question and answer dialogue is the dynamic that provides momentum throughout Malachi. The questions are asked in alternating modes by Israel (1:2, 7 moving the plot), the prophet (2:10, 15 rhetorical), and Israel (2:17, 3:8, 13 moving the plot). See Craig, "Interrogatives in Haggai-Zechariah," 227.

2. חזקו עלי דבריכם has been variously translated: "you use strong, arrogant words" (Koehler/Baumgartner), "your words have been stout" (KJV, RSV), "you have spoken harsh words" (NRSV). For a similar construction see 2 Sam 24:4.

3. אז (v.16) "then" changed by text editors to זה or זאת "this, these things" based on LXX reading ταῦτα (so JPS and Jerusalem Bible). The change implies that the doubts are spoken by those who fear Yahweh. The MT involves assigning the foregoing doubts

those expressing the shame of vain service exercise a communal discipline of faithful discernment and recommitment to the "fear of the Lord". God takes note of this discipline and responds with a promise of protection on the Day of the Lord when the issue at the heart of the complaint—God's inability to judge between human behavior—will be resolved decidedly in favor of the "two ways" formula. "Then once more you shall see the difference between the righteous and the wicked, between one who serves God and one who does not serve him" (Mal 3:18).

In understanding the import of this striking parallel, it will be helpful to set it within the context of recent canon studies. It is well known that the Hebrew Bible is organized into three large blocks of Law, Prophets and Writings. A growing body of scholarship substantiates the view that the basic grammar of Israel's faith is contained in the Law and Prophets, while the Writings are a reflection on this core.[4] Taking account of this canonical ordering means that interpreters need to be sensitive to associations between the blocks of the Writings and the Law-Prophets that indicate parallel lines of thought. The existence of such parallels provides opportunities for the interpreter to expand a theme through probing the resonances

---

to the godless in Israel and the words of the God-fearers are left unspoken. But this is thematically unsuitable. In both 3:13 and 16 the righteous speak among themselves. According to 3:13, Yahweh refuses to listen to their words; he finds them intolerable. It is inconceivable that these same words should now elicit a favorable response from him. Yahweh's contrasting reactions suggest that the tone of the God-fearers words changed, a change presaged by the particle אז, revising their assessment. See Glazier-McDonald, *Malachi*, 217.

4 For a summary of evidence that supports the position that the "minor prophets" were always considered as one Book of the Twelve, see Nogalski, "The Redactional Shaping of Nahum 1," 193–94.

For canonical discussion, see Seitz, *The Goodly Fellowship of the Prophets*, 56, 105–26. This position does not imply conclusions about the dating of individual books, only their function. Nor does it mean that the Writings enjoy a diminished canonical status vis-à-vis the Law and Prophets. The issue of the order of books in the Old Testament is complex. The history of Jewish, Protestant, Roman Catholic and Eastern Orthodox Bibles contains several variants in order. The present order, treating the Book of the Twelve as a single book and placing it last was fixed in the West during the 16th and 17th centuries. Seitz comments, "It has no known exemplar before the modern period." "Canon, Narrative, and the Old Testament's Literal Sense,'" 29. Theological considerations figured heavily in this decision. John Calvin's preface to Malachi is typical: "[H]e was no doubt one of the Prophets, and, as it appears, the last; for at the end of his Book he exhorts the people to continue in their adherence to the pure doctrine of the law: and his he did, because God was not afterwards to send Prophets in succession as before; for it was his purpose that the Jews should have s stronger desire for Christ, they having been for a time without any Prophets." *Commentaries on the Twelve Minor Prophets*, 468.

created between divisions of the canon. This investigation restricts itself to the associations between the Book of the Twelve and the Psalms.

Malachi concludes the Prophets, and Psalms begins the Writings. Thus Malachi and Psalms constitute the seam that links the Writings with the divisions of the Prophets and the Law, and as such have a special relationship to each other. We are concerned, initially, with the striking association between Malachi and Psalms on the crisis provoked by an expression of shame as the experience of failed expectations. This association will raise additional questions about the relationship between the Book of the Twelve and the Psalms and, derivatively, whether other instances of association between the Book of the Twelve and Psalms exist. We will address briefly these additional questions at the conclusion of this section.

The interpretative force of the seam between Malachi and Psalms can be exposed more clearly by paying attention to the ending of Malachi. Many commentators interpret Mal 3:13–24 (Eng. 3:13—4:6) as a later addition, noting especially how the citing of Moses 3:22 (Eng. 4:4) and Elijah 3:23 (Eng. 4:5) rounds out the book with the endorsement of the Law and the Prophets.[5] While this is a helpful insight, more attention needs to be paid to the contribution of Mal 3:13–21 (Eng. 3:13—4:3) to the concluding endorsements. It is an expanded modification of similar charge against God in Mal 2:17—3:5. In this text the prophet makes the complaint on behalf of God ("you have spoken against me") against the people's wearisome complaining: "Every one who does evil is good in the sight of the Lord, and he delights in them." God responds to the charge "Where is the God of justice?" God sends a messenger of the covenant who embodies God's swift witness against evil doers and who reasserts the divine constant of the possibility of life for those who return to God.

This text has been reshaped in Mal 3:13–18 in three ways. First, the prophet's charge against the people in 2:17 "You have wearied the Lord" now appears at 3:13 as divine speech "You have spoken harsh words against me."

Second, the people's charge against God in 2:17 "Every one who does evil is good in the sight of the Lord, and he delights in them . . . Where is the God of justice?" is restated at 3:14 in evaluative language: "It is *vain*[6] to

---

5. For example Redditt, "The Production and Reading," 24, and Schart, "Reconstructing the Redactional History," 45.

6. שוא in the sense of absence of trustworthiness (see, *inter alia*: Deut 5:20; Job 7:3, 11:11, 15:31, 31:5; Ps 12:2, 24:4, 26:4, 31:6, 60:11, 144:8,11; Prov 30:8; Hos 10:4; Jonah 2:8; Zech 10:2).

serve God. What do we *profit*[7] by keeping his command or by going about as mourners before the Lord of Hosts? Now we *count* the arrogant blessed;[8] evildoers not only prosper, but when they put God to the test they escape." This is an activity of discernment that yields convictions exactly opposite to the promises God has attached to covenantal piety.[9]

Third, the messenger component of Mal 3:1–2 is absent in the reshaped text; the messenger is now transferred at 4:5 to Elijah who appears at the advent of the great and terrible day of the Lord.[10] In the absence of the messenger to set things right in 3:2b–4, the resolution phase in the reshaped text is initiated by religious activity as "those who revered the Lord spoke with one another . . . and thought on his name." This activity is contrasted to the initial negative conclusions. God's declaration to resolve the complaint and reaffirm the validity of the "two ways" is predicated on this communal discipline that results in renewed faith.

Compared with Mal 2:17—3:5, Mal 3:13–18 uses wisdom-like motifs to describe widespread cynicism and to reiterate God's faithfulness. We see these motifs in two instances. (1) The use of evaluative language supports the activity of discernment that reaches conclusions exactly opposite to God's promise. Whereas in Mal 3:12 God had promised "all the nations call you honored (*'ashre*)," only three verses later God's people pronounce the arrogant blessed (*'ashre*).[11] (2) More telling is the double description of those who find a way back to trusting in God in Mal 3:16, "those who revered the Lord spoke with one another" and "those who revered the Lord and thought on his name." The intriguing phrase לחשבי שמו "those who thought on his name" has no parallel in the Old Testament, but a similar phrase is found in Ps 119:59 "When I think of your ways, I turn my feet to your testimonies." This discipline of torah piety moving from thought to commitment parallels similar ways of the God-fearers in Mal 3:15–16 and in Ps 73:16 (לדעת ואחשבה "but when I thought to understand . . . I went to the sanctuary").

---

7. בצע in the sense of self-interested gain (Job 22:3; Ps 30:9; Prov 1:19, 15:27, 28:16; Isa 56:11; Jer 6:13, 8:1; Ezek 22:27; Hab 2:19).

8. מאשרים piel participle of אשר "to call blessed" (Gen 30:13; Job 29:11; Ps 72:17; Prov 31:28; Song 6:9; Mal 3:12).

9. This is forcefully underscored by Mal 3:15 undercutting Mal 3:12.

10. See Berry, "Malachi's Dual Design," 269, and Redditt, "Zechariah 9–14, Malachi," 254.

11. For translating *'ashre* as "honorable," see Hanson, "'How Honorable!' How Shameful.'"

This comparison between Mal 2:17—3:5 and 3:13–24 (Eng. 3:13—4:6) suggests that the later version participates in what G. T. Sheppard has called "the sapientializing of the Old Testament"[12] in which wisdom became a hermeneutical construct, guiding scribal sages in their task of canon-making.[13] If Moses symbolizes the Law and Elijah the Prophets, can it be that Malachi's expression of shame and the resolution of its theological crisis by discernment and reconfirmation of the "two ways" is the product of its "seaming" with the wisdom-like nature of Ps 73?

To summarize, the division of the Prophets closes with Malachi's description of shame as an unsettled question, provoking a rare disclosure of God's stake in the crisis. This description finds an extended reflection in Pss 73–75. It is notable that the religious activity of the people of God in the chapter that closes the second section of the Hebrew canon comprises an ongoing dialogue of three parts: continued confrontation with the raw facts of shame experienced as God's reneging on God's promises, the intense struggle of befuddled believers to regain commitment, and God's promise to uphold the validity of the two ways. This is the final word from the Prophets, reaffirmed and expanded in the Psalms, on the religious experience of God's people engaged in an ongoing struggle to live faithfully in the midst of pressure to lapse into moral cynicism.[14] Significantly this word also establishes the foundation for anticipating a new Day of the Lord.[15]

The Book of the Twelve and the Psalter

The striking association between Mal 3:13–18 with Ps 73 encourages us to inquire more broadly about the relation between the Book of the Twelve and the Psalter since these two books sit next to each other as the seam between the Prophets and the Writings. Seitz has recently pointed out that "Jonah and Habakkuk contain a kind of speech-form unusual in the prophetic books and in the mouths of the prophets especially. This form is the

---

12. Sheppard, *Wisdom as a Hermeneutical Construct*, 13.

13. Van Leeuwen, "Scribal Wisdom and Theodicy," 31.

14. This statement is made strictly on canonical placement and independently from questions of the historical provenance of the Book of the Twelve.

15. As Seitz has pointed out, "the heart of canonical reading . . . is that aspect of God's word to Israel which continues to press for a hearing and addresses new generations with an old word, borne of a specific time and specific application, and without shedding that, mov[es] forward through time to enclose new readers and new situations." "On Letting a Text 'Act Like a Man,'" 167.

Shame as a Theological Crisis

psalm."[16] To the examples of Jonah 2:2–9 and Hab 3:1–19 can be added the well-known psalm-fragments of Amos 4:11; 5:8–9; 9:5–6;[17] and Nah 1:3b–5.[18] The cumulative effect supports Seitz' observation: "The fact that Habakkuk's prayer is presented with the identical rubrics ('On *shigionoth*'; 'for the director of music. On my stringed instruments'), as in the psalms, means to direct the reader to that 150-prayer book. This book seeks to inculcate, through prayer, the attitude of discernment necessary for comprehending the lessons of history, as God and no journalistic technique can reveal. The link beyond the Twelve to the Psalter is a form of canonical shaping as well."[19]

We have described the way Ps 73 comments on Mal 3. Another example of a reverberation with Ps 73 is Zephaniah. The two share vivid mockings of the impotence of God (Ps 73:11 and Zeph 1:12), expressions of betrayal (Ps 73:1–2 and Zeph 3:7) and the movement beyond shame into praise. (Ps 73:21–26 and Zeph 3:19)

Moving to other psalms, interesting connections are suggested by the association of Amos 9:2–4a with Ps 139:7–12. These texts share the pattern of the four-fold schematization of the universe (heaven, underworld, earth, and sea).[20] But whereas Amos employs the pattern to intensify the impossibility of escaping God's judgment, the psalm uses the pattern to underscore the universality of God's providential care.[21] The negative conclusion of Amos is reversed by a more hopeful comment in Ps 139. The psalm also comments positively on the experience of Jonah in fleeing from the presence of God. (1:3,10)[22] Jonah's prayer from the belly of the great fish is echoed through multiple psalms.[23]

16. Ibid., 170.

17. Wolff, *Joel and Amos*, 215–17.

18. Gerstenberger asks the questions: "Have these psalmic elements been placed in the context of prophetic utterances and discourses by mistake? Or imagining the opposite extreme: do the liturgical components constitute the original matrix of communal interaction out of which have grown prophetic sayings and speeches?" See his "Psalms in the Book of the Twelve," 72–89, esp. 73. While these are interesting questions regarding composition and setting of the Twelve, our concern is with the resonances between the Twelve as a block and the Psalter.

19. Seitz, *Prophecy and Hermeneutics*, 215.

20. Wolff, *Joel and Amos*, 341, and Mays, *Amos*, 154, point to the pattern's roots in a widespread hymnic tradition of the ancient Near East.

21. Hossfeld and Zenger, *Psalmen*, 101–50, 723.

22. Ibid., 722, also 730 for the psalm's relationship with Jeremiah.

23. Jonah 2:3//Pss 120:1 and 130:1; Jonah 2:4//Ps 42:7; Jonah 2:5//Ps 36:22 and 5:7;

Regarding the three hymnic fragments of Amos, their common affirmation of the Lord is King provides a fruitful node for commentary by psalms from Book V. Careful study of the interrelations between the Book of the Twelve and the Psalter will reveal additional opportunities for realizing how the Prophets look to the Writings for amplification, commentary, and reflection upon their message.

SHAME IN THE BOOK OF THE TWELVE

Recent study of Malachi's place within the Book of the Twelve has underscored its function as the concluding piece of an overarching framework that provides a hermeneutical perspective from which to interpret the Book of the Twelve as literary theology.[24] Indeed, several motifs of the resolution of shame in Mal 3:13–18 make an *inclusio* with material in Hosea, the beginning of this hermeneutical framework.[25] The call in Hos 14:3 (Eng. 14:2) to "Take words with you and return to the Lord" forecasts the actions of those who in Mal 3:16 "spoke with one another . . . and thought on his name" as they struggled with the shame of experiencing failed expectations. The concluding verse of Hos 14:10 (Eng. 14:9) "Those who are wise understand these things; those who are discerning know them. For the ways of the Lord are right, and the upright walk in them, but transgressors stumble in them." points this entire collection of prophecy in the direction of its ongoing use by the wise to discern the unshakable validity of the "two ways." This perspective on the Book of the Twelve receives final endorsement in Mal 3:18

Jonah 2:6//Ps 69:1; Jonah 2:7//Pss 30:3 and 16:10; Jonah 2:10//Pss 22:26 and 3:8.

24. See Deist, "Parallels and Reinterpretation in the Book of Joel"; Seitz, "What Lesson Will History Teach?" 462–66; Redditt, "Zechariah 9–14," 272: "All reflections of canonical theology in Malachi indicate to a greater or lesser degree (1) the book's dependence on scripture or (2) the book's awareness of scripture or (3) the awareness by the producer(s) of the book of the general situation reflected in writings of the same age as Malachi . . . [T]he broader and more diverse the reflection of previous writings, the stronger the confirmation of the claim that Malachi closes a chapter in the development of canon . . . Malachi's evaluation takes place in its canonical context. Whether or not the writer, editor, or redactor intentionally encoded each allusion, each correspondence to biblical texts merits acceptance as part of a network of images orienting the message of Malachi within its 'position' as part of the Christian scriptures, the Hebrew Bible, the minor prophets, and any specialized section within these divisions. For such purposes, concepts from the domain of comparative literary studies, such as dependence, influence, allusion, and intertextuality, serve as essential tools."

25. See Petersen, *Zechariah and Malachi*, 232.

where God promises to those who revere and think on God's name, "you shall distinguish between the righteous and the wicked."[26]

Joel's placement in the order of the Book of the Twelve contributes to the interpretive framework of the entire collection as well.[27] Joel brings the important theme of the Day of the Lord into the framework.[28] The advent of the Day of the Lord, with its twice repeated promise "my people shall never again be put to shame" (2:26–27), actually begins with the onslaught of a "day . . . great, terrible indeed—who can endure it?" (2:11). Yet in defiance of this crisis, an evangelical call to a liturgy of repentance "with fasting, with weeping, and with mourning" (2:12) stimulates the ministers of the Lord to weep and say, "Why should it be said among the peoples, 'Where is their God?'" (2:17). Israel pleads with God to avoid being tormented in defeat with the evidence of God's impotence which exacerbates their shame.

The beginning of Joel's call to repentance: "return to me with all your heart, with fasting, with weeping and with mourning . . . return to the Lord, your God" (2:12–13) amplifies a similar call in Hos 14:2–3 (Eng. 14:1–2), which appears to be a part of the hermeneutical framework of the Book of the Twelve: "Return, O Israel, to the Lord your God . . . Take words with you and return to the Lord."[29] Joel also contributes to the framework the element of God's resolution of the experience of being put to shame. God responds to those who participate in the liturgy of repentance: "You shall eat in plenty and be satisfied and praise the name of the Lord your God . . . and my people shall never again be put to shame.[30] You shall know that I am in the midst of Israel . . . and my people shall never again be put to shame" (2:26–27). God's sending "grain, wine, and oil" (Joel 2:19) restores

---

26. Redditt, "Zechariah 9–14," 255. Steck, *The Prophetic Books*, 61, and 61–85, summarizes extensive research showing that concluding chapters to prophetic books are "statements of purpose in the flow" of such books as Isaiah and the Twelve.

27. Nogalski, "Joel as 'Literary Anchor,'" 107.

28. See Rendtorff, "How to Read the Book of the Twelve," 77, and Schart, "Reconstructing," 58, 62–63.

29. Wolff notes that 14:2 (Eng. 14:1) is "unlike the exhortations in 2:4f; 4:15; 8:5a (cj.) . . . the purpose here is not to snatch Israel away from a threatening judgment. The disaster has already taken place." *Hosea*, 234. See also Nogalski, "Joel as 'Literary Anchor,'" 96.

30. The motifs of not being put to shame and praising the name of the Lord are taken up again in Zeph 3:9–20. See chapter 1 for a discussion of praise and not being put to shame in Pss 73–75.

The Self-Shaming God Who Reconciles

"the grain, the wine, and the oil" (Hos 2:10–14, Eng. 2:8–12) which God has taken away in judgment.[31]

The motif of being able to enjoy the fruits of one's labor is a common metaphor for not being put to shame. Psalm 37:19 comments on the blameless "they are not put to shame in evil times, in the days of famine they have abundance." Conversely, not being able to enjoy the fruits of one's labor is a metaphor for being put to shame.[32]

This figure of speech is used throughout the Book of the Twelve. Thus Amos describes God's putting Israel to shame in 5:11 "You have built houses of hewn stone, but you shall not dwell in them; you have planted pleasant vineyards, but you shall not drink their wine," with the result that "In all the vineyards there shall be wailing, for I will pass through the midst of you, says the Lord" (5:17). In the final chapter of Amos the day of the Lord is an occasion for radical judgment and restoration (9:9–13). On that day the judgments of 5:11 are reversed, "they shall rebuild the ruined cities and inhabit them; they shall plant vineyards and drink their wine, and they shall make gardens and eat their fruit" (9:14). The final verse of the chapter states that the assurance of this expectation is founded upon God's never being put to shame again. "I will plant them upon their land, and they shall never again be plucked up out of the land which I have given them" (9:15). Zeph 1:12–13 quotes Amos 5:11 in meting out judgment upon those who say, "The Lord will not do good, nor will he do ill." The motif is again repeated in Hag 1:5–6 and 2:16–17 where Amos 4:9 is quoted, "I smote you and all the products of your toil with blight and mildew and hail; yet you did not return to me."

In parallel to material expectations, the negative results from calling upon God also connote the experience of shame. Micah 3:1–4 excoriates corrupt leaders and pronounces the judgment: "Then they will cry to the Lord, but he will not answer them." A similar fate awaits mercenary prophets in 3:5–8: "Therefore . . . the seers shall be disgraced and the diviners put to shame; they shall all cover their lips, for there is no answer from God." See also Zech 7:13–14.

Habakkuk paints a significant picture of counter-intuitive faith in 3:17–19 that rejoices "Though the fig tree do not blossom, nor fruit be

---

31. For a discussion of the theme of God's withholding and returning the fruits of the land in Hosea, see Braaten, "God Sows: Hosea's Land Theme," 104–32.

32. For the location of this metaphor as a "futility curse" within a covenantal setting, see Hillers, *Treaty Curses*, 28–29.

on the vines . . ." (clearly a time of shame) because "God, the Lord, is my strength." This is a sentiment that Ps 73:26 underscores, "My flesh and my heart may fail, but God is the strength (Hebrew "rock") of my heart and my portion for ever."

Seen in the light of this framework, Mal 3:13–18 is the final example in the Prophets of the call of Hosea and Joel to return and God's promise to resolve the shame of betrayal. The speakers in Mal 3:14 question, "What do we profit . . . by going about as mourners before the Lord of hosts?" Out of their shame, induced by God's inability to rule, they challenge the usefulness of Joel's call to walk about as mourners, that is, to "return to the Lord, your God." However, in Mal 3:16 religious activity of some formal nature does occur that yields renewed faith which is sealed by God's blessing of protection on the day of the Lord when the reliability of the "two ways" will be demonstrated.

A similar note is struck in Mic 7. Micah is the central book in the Book of the Twelve, and its last chapter is an especially important statement of thematic material seen across the collection. The chapter begins with a lengthy catalogue of how humans betray the expectations of sibling, neighbor, friend, spouse, parents, and associates. Indeed the chapter is a catalogue of shame experienced by one who struggles to be faithful to God. The betrayers act with impunity, and their taunt, "Where is the Lord your God?" (7:10) exposes their intent to provoke shame by mocking God's power to rule. Contrastingly, the shamed ones wait patiently on the Lord for deliverance, and when that comes, the betrayers' impunity will be of no help, and they will be covered with shame. Mic 7 is a keystone in the interpretative framework of the Book of the Twelve.[33]

The correspondence between Hosea/Joel and Malachi combined with the extended discussion of betrayal and vindication in Micah has the effect of setting the interpretation of each document of the Book of the Twelve within a framework.[34] Within this framework serious challenges are

---

33. For critical issues concerning Mic 7, see Kessler, *Micah*, 296.

34. This approach differs from a type of canonical reading advocated by Conrad, *Reading the Latter Prophets*. He attempts to read the individual books in the Book of the Twelve in the light of Isaiah, Jeremiah, and Ezekiel. This approach continues to treat each book discretely, thus blocking any understanding of the unity of the Twelve. Our approach also differs from a descriptive investigation of "themes" that recur throughout the Book of the Twelve where no attention is paid to a structure that exercises some control over the variety of ways each theme is voiced throughout the collection. For example, see Nogalski, "Recurring Themes in the Book of the Twelve," 125–36.

directed at the integrity of God and the reliability of God's rule. The recurring question is: Can God maintain the validity of the "two ways" before God's people in the face of formidable hostility? Is it the fate of the faithful to be put to shame on the basis of God's impotence? The resounding affirmation of the sovereignty of God and God's comforting promise to God's people of not being put to shame is the pivotal message around which the Book of the Twelve coalesces. This message the wise and discerning will heed and will return to the Lord with renewed faith.

THE THEOLOGICAL CRISIS IN THE BOOK OF THE TWELVE

Those who put the Book of the Twelve into its final shape made it into a theological document that laid the foundation for faithful obedience to God in conditions hostile to such obedience. Central to this foundation is the demonstration of the integrity of God. That this is an overriding issue becomes clearer when attention is paid to another element of the hermeneutical framework of the Book of the Twelve: the self-designation formula for God. The base text for this exposition of the name of God is Exod 34:6–7.

> The Lord, the Lord,
> a God merciful and gracious,
> slow to anger,
> and abounding in steadfast love and faithfulness,
> keeping steadfast love for the thousandth generation,
> forgiving iniquity and transgression and sin,
> yet by no means clearing the guilty,
> but visiting the iniquity of the parents
> upon the children
> and the children's children,
> to the third and the fourth generation.

The self-designation formula shows up most clearly in the Book of the Twelve at the key-stone position of the collection in Mic 7:18–20 which brings that book to a climactic end and in the beginning of the following book in Nah 1:2–3a.[35] This double statement provides the pivot point

---

35. This extended peroration reaches backward and forward. It answers the taunting of Mic 7:10 "Where is the Lord your God?" and substantiates the shame of the judgment of the perpetrators of the shame of vv. 2–6. It reaches forward to under gird the rhetorical questions that challenge hubris in Nah 1.6 "Who can stand before his indignation? Who can endure the heat of his anger?" It is striking that Micah contains three of the seven cited instances of cynical and hubristic speech against God.

around which the separate writings of the collection are turned into a coherent message.

> Who is a God like you, pardoning iniquity
> and passing over transgression
> for the remnant of your possession?
> He does not retain his anger for ever
> because he delights in showing clemency.
> He will again have compassion upon us,
> he will tread our iniquities under foot.
> You will cast all our sins
> into the depths of the sea.
> You will show faithfulness to Jacob
> and unswerving loyalty to Abraham,
> as you have sworn to our ancestors from the days of old.
> A jealous and avenging God is the Lord,
> the Lord is avenging and wrathful;
> the Lord takes vengeance on his adversaries
> and rages against his enemies.
> The Lord is slow to anger but great in power,
> and the Lord will by no means clear the guilty.

Clearly the dialectic between justice and mercy which is at the heart of who God is in Exod 34 receives a powerful restatement at the mid-point of the Book of the Twelve.

In addition, the self-designation formula figures prominently in the call to repentance in Joel 2:12–14: "Return to the Lord, your God, for he is gracious and merciful, slow to anger, and abounding in steadfast love, and relents of punishing. Who knows whether he will not turn and relent, and leave a blessing behind him?"

In the book of Jonah, this self-designation formula gets pushed to the extreme as doomed Ninevites, who have no knowledge at all of God's character, nevertheless gamble on the possibility of God's repenting of evil when presented with their profound repentance ("Who knows, God may relent and turn from his fierce anger, so that we do not perish." Jonah 3:9) The call to repentance extends to not only humans but also to animals being covered in sackcloth and joining in a plea for mercy. (Jonah 3:7-8) This ridiculous touch, however, is clarified when it is seen as a literalization of the metaphor in Joel 1:18a and 20a ("How the cattle moan! . . . Even the wild animals pant for you.").[36] Conversely, Jonah's pique at Nineveh's deliverance

---

36 Cooper, "In Praise of Divine Caprice," 161.

becomes more unseemly when his cry for deliverance from the belly of the whale (itself a literalization of the metaphor "From the belly of Sheol I cried out") was heeded.

God's reprieve becomes the centerpiece of Jonah's complaint against God in 4:2, repeating the words of Joel: "for I knew that you are a gracious God and merciful, slow to anger, and abounding in steadfast love, and ready to relent from punishing."[37] Not knowing God's character, the Ninevites nevertheless desperately hope and are not disappointed. The parable of the creation of the bush that flourishes for a day and then is cut down by God, clouding Jonah's fate, is finally a defense of God's character to show concern (!) over the fate of Nineveh. This pushing one side of God's character to the point of parody in Jonah upsets the tension that exists between God's mercy and holiness. This tension is restored in Nahum, the companion book to Jonah, which celebrates the destruction of Assyria.[38]

In the fourteen instances where the self-designation formula is quoted in the Old Testament, four occur in the Book of the Twelve.[39] The formula motivates a liturgy of repentance in Joel, is restated in exuberant praise and sobering warning at the juncture of Micah—Nahum, and is the basis of Jonah's assault on God's integrity. Its occurrence at strategic places over a range of disparate literature testifies to the importance attached to its explication of the integrity of God within a body of literature that has all the marks of speaking to conditions that threaten that integrity.

For example, the Book of the Twelve contains several examples of cynical and hubristic speech directed at God: "We have no king, for we fear not the Lord, and a king, what could he do for us?" (Hos 10:3), "Evil shall not overtake or meet us" (Amos 9:10), and "Who will bring me down to the ground?" (Obad 3).[40]

---

37. Dozeman, "Inner-biblical Interpretation," 207–23, investigates the mutual relationship between Joel and Jonah. For a study of the relationship between Jonah and Micah-Nahum, see Cooper, "In Praise of Divine Caprice," 144–92. I differ with Cooper on his construal of God's freedom as "caprice." The self-designation formula originates in a covenantal setting.

38. See Childs, *Introduction of the Old Testament*, 425–26.

39. Dentan, "Literary Affinities of Exodus XXXIV 6f." 34, sees the formula as the product of the School of the Wise Men. If so, then it might be the final theological stamp of the canon. Bosman, "The Paradoxical Presence of Exodus 34:6–7," 233–43, lists a total of 27 instances of full quotation and partial allusions.

40. One is struck by the blatant certainty of these statements of God's impotence. This has prompted Brueggeman's suggestion that we interpret them as coming from "reservoirs of unreason" that lie deep beneath human consciousness and shape thinking

Shame as a Theological Crisis

Three examples occur in Micah: "Disgrace will not overtake us. Is the Lord's patience exhausted?[41] Is this how he acts?" (2:6–7), "Is not the Lord in the midst of us? No evil shall come upon us" (3:11), and "Where is the Lord your God?" (7:10).[42] Against such concentrated hostility, the keystone to the Book of the Twelve (Mic 7:18–20, Nah 1:2–3a) stands as a contradiction.

In Zephaniah God's power is mocked by those who say, "The Lord will not do good, nor will he do ill"[43] (1:12). These mockers are called the "proudly exultant ones" (3:11) and the solidity of their self-reliance repels the force of God's justice designed to bring about remorse and repentance. (3:3–5, 7) In Zephaniah the intransigence of self-reliance and self-dealing renders God's acts of justice as failures and puts to shame the expectation of God for a return to obedience.[44] The description of the shamers of God as exultant (עליז) is also how Zephaniah excoriates Nineveh in the woe oracle against Assyria (2:13–15).[45] The proudly exultant mockers are part and parcel of the exultant city Nineveh "that dwelt secure, that said to herself, 'I am and there is none else'" (2:15).[46] Thus Nineveh's mocking informs and thickens the mocking of God's people.

---

in destructive ways. See his treatment of three citations of hubristic speech in Micah, "Voices of the Night—Against Justice," 20–24, and "Reservoirs of Unreason," 99–104.

41. This reference to the Lord's patience recalls what must have been familiar to all, the self-designation formula of Exod 34:6 "The Lord . . . patient and abounding in steadfast love." Here the rapacious are using the self-designation formula to frame their hubris as a sign of the Lord's blessing! See Mays, *Micah*, 70 and Hillers, *Micah*, 36.

42. See the discussion of Wolff, "The Unmasking Word," 35–48.

43. Széles, *Wrath and Mercy*, 85, "This conclusion casts doubt on Yahweh's creative power and degrades the living God to the level of idols."

44. God's statement, "I said, 'Surely she will fear me, she will accept correction' . . . but all the more they were eager to make all their deeds corrupt" (3:7) is repeated in Ps 73:1–2. Both statements begin with the particle אך ("surely") expressing a confident expectation which is then followed by a particle which signals a stunning reversal (אכן in Zeph 3:7 and י with the first person pronoun in Ps 73:2). See Muraoka, *Emphatic Words and Structures in Biblical Hebrew*, 129–30, 132. For other instances of this theme of human intransigence shaming God in the Book of the Twelve, see Amos' "liturgy of wasted opportunity" (4:6–12) and Hos 11. Crenshaw, "A Liturgy of Wasted Opportunity," 27–37, interprets the rebuffed judgments of God as opportunities for repentance which humans squandered. I see it differently as Amos' demonstration of the inability of humans to repent which can be overcome only by God's eschatological deliverance (Amos 9:13–15).

45. עליז describing a city is used elsewhere only in Isa 22:2; 23:7; 32:13.

46. Isa 47:8, 10 uses a variation of this phrase to describe Babylon. Széles, *Wrath and Mercy*, 99, calls this expression of self-divination "potential lunacy."

The Self-Shaming God Who Reconciles

Zephaniah links the mocking of God with God's failure to effect justice (3:5). Within the Book of the Twelve, Zephaniah adds urgency to the cry in Malachi of believers who have been put to shame: "Where is the God of justice?" (2:17) and "when they [the evildoers] put God to the test they escape" (3:15). Zephaniah prophesies that the great destruction on the Day of the Lord will put to shame the self-reliance of those who mock God's power (1:18) by bringing upon them the futility curse (1:13).[47] On that Day, through a thorough-going cleansing of the proudly exultant ones, God will cease putting to shame (3:11) a remnant of God's people by God causing to flourish reverence (3:9), integrity (3:13), peace (3:15) and praise (3:19).[48]

In the light of these challenges, we can see how the Book of the Twelve has been shaped into a powerful exposition of the preservation of God's purpose to be of everlasting benefit to God's people. "For I the Lord do not change; therefore you, O children of Jacob, are not consumed . . . Return to me, and I will return to you, says the Lord of hosts . . . Then all nations will call you blessed, for you will be a land of delight, says the Lord of hosts" (Mal 3:6, 7, 12).

This is the background for understanding the presentation of the theological stake in the crisis of Mal 3:13–18. Can God continue to be counted on being the God of justice and mercy? The accusation of those who speak harshly "Henceforth we deem the arrogant blessed" (Mal 3:15) is a direct contradiction of God's promise, "all nations will call you blessed" (Mal 3:12). Indeed, God's declaration to uphold how God speaks of God's self is the foundation that supports the solid reaffirmation of the validity of the "two ways." Might not this self-designation formula have formed the substance of the God-fearers' speaking and thinking on God's name?[49]

---

47. See Berlin, *Zephaniah*, 131, commenting on Zeph 3:5: "the noun *Bšt* which occurs also in 3:19, and the verb *Bwš*, in 3:11, are not limited to English 'to be ashamed,' but include also 'reproach, disgrace, condemn, discomfit, confound.' The sense is not that the subject of this verb will feel shame, but that he or she will be disgraced, condemned, or confounded." See also her comments on Zeph 3:11, ibid., 135.

48. Compare the change of shame into praise in Ps 73:25–26.

49. See also Joel 2:17. Canonical criticism helps to flesh out the discipline of covenantal faithfulness in Mal 3:13–17. The conclusion of vanity in Mal 3:13–14 leads to weariness as we know from Ps 73:16. This weariness is called out by God in the controversy that the Lord has with his people in Mic 6:3 "How have I wearied you?" The intention of God's reproach of Israel is to motivate them to "know the saving acts of the Lord" (Mic 6:5). Thus Micah suggests that what might have occurred in the community's "thinking on his name" in Mal 3:16 was a reconfirmation of the saving acts of the Lord. This is in opposition to Crenshaw's position of the book of remembrance as a "heavenly

Shame as a Theological Crisis

This collection of testimonies points to a sustained struggle to be faithful. Joel's liturgy of repentance, Micah's counsel to wait patiently for vindication, Habakkuk's model of counter-intuitive rejoicing, Malachi's description of a community's discipline and, negatively, Jonah's disappointment over God's graciousness, provide snapshots in a tableaux of faithful struggle against conditions that give rise to doubt and shame.[50] This becomes a witness for the wise and discerning in cleaving to upholding the rule of God.[51]

The promise God makes to readers of the Hebrew Bible is that there will be a day on which "you shall distinguish between the righteous and the wicked, between one who serves God and one who does not serve him." For those whose names are in the "book of remembrance" (Mal 3:18), this promised day becomes the basis of enduring hope. In the next chapter we follow the struggle to live beyond shame into the New Testament as that struggle is waged within the Trinitarian understanding of God.

---

book [containing] the names of those who have trusted Yahweh in spite of everything and when justice will finally dawn on earth." Malachi's community does not sacrifice present reality by gazing into the future. It confronts reality by remembering and trusting in the record of God's acts. Crenshaw, "Theodicy in the Book of the Twelve," 186.

50. Of the three endorsements that make up the concluding framework for the Book of the Twelve, only one addresses at any length a burning issue for the community that reveres this writing. It is the Writings with its perennial issue of shame and shame's associated theological questions. Could it be possible that the Law and the Prophets are meant to be interpreted from the vantage point of the Writings as well?

51. See Seitz, *Prophecy and History*, 214–15. Nasuti makes the helpful distinction between the "point of view" of a biblical text and its "point of standing." Point of view is principally concerned with the perspective discerned within the plot of the text, while point of standing addresses the response intended to be elicited from the reader. For details see, "The Poetics of Biblical Prophecy," 112–13. Within the category of point of standing would fall the directive to the reader of Hos 14:1–2, 9; the expressions of awe in Mic 7:18–20—Nah 1:1–6; and the example of Mal 3:16–18.

4

Living Beyond Shame within the Christian Canon

We take as foundational the shape of the Christian canon, comprised of two testaments. Each testament speaks in its own right and in conversation with the other. This conversation is crucial to the theological interpretation of Scripture. Christopher R. Seitz sums up this dialectic of canonical interpretation. The plain sense of the text of the Old Testament extends "beyond itself because of the challenge of rendering the subject matter, which now entails a second accorded witness." The Old Testament's voice is allowed to stand to ensure that "the New Testament's emphases remain rooted in the soil from which they have sprung."[1]

The struggle described in the Old Testament to live faithfully under conditions that produce shame over God's impotence are barely beneath the surface of the great hymn of expectation that sets the context for the birth of Jesus.[2]

> Blessed be the Lord God of Israel,
>   for he has visited and redeemed his people,
> and has raised up a horn of salvation for us
>   in the house of his servant David,
> as he spoke by the mouth of his holy prophets from of old,
>   that we should be saved from our enemies,
>   and from the hand of all who hate us;

---

1. "The Canonical Approach and Theological Interpretation," 58–108, esp. 80, 88. See also a helpful summary in Goldingay, "Old Testament Theology and the Canon," 17–26.

2. For a convenient access to the vast literature on infancy narratives, see Brown, *The Birth of the Messiah*.

> to perform the mercy promised to our fathers,
> and to remember his holy covenant,
> the oath which he swore to our father Abraham,
> to grant us that we, being delivered from the hand of our enemies,
> might serve him without fear. (Luke 1:68–74)

Consequently, when Jesus came preaching

> The Spirit of the Lord is upon me,
> because he has anointed me to preach good news to the poor.
> He has sent me to proclaim release to the captives
> and recovering of sight to the blind,
> to set at liberty those who are oppressed,
> to proclaim the acceptable year of the Lord. (Luke 4:18–19)

his claims of the closest of divine sponsorship and authority invited his hearers to cast their trust wholly upon him and his mission.

The passion of Christ, particularly in its synoptic arrangement, utterly destroys this trust. Matthew (and Mark) describe the cruelest of ironies that the Messiah himself should give voice to the most hellish of experiences of theological shame as Jesus is broken on the cross. As is well known, Luke's account has no similar scene of Jesus being broken. Luke does, however, record how the impact of witnessing the defeat of God's anointed throws his followers into the profound shame of mistaken trust in Jesus. We will now survey this synoptic material.

In the Gospel of Matthew, Jesus' claims of trust in God are what is being ridiculed in the taunting from those who stood around his cross. "He trusts in God; let God deliver him now, if he wants to; for he said, 'I am God's Son'" (Matt 27:43). The cry of dereliction from the cross, "My God, my God, why have you forsaken me?" (v. 46) resonates with the cries in the psalms of those who have experienced the withdrawal of the *Deus praesens*.[3] The gospel writer is quoting from Ps 22:1,8 where the supplicant is expressing shame through what is experienced as God's forfeiture of

---

3. It is significant that the one who is abandoned by God in Ps 22 intensifies the experience of abandonment through recalling the ancestors who cried to God and were saved, who trusted in God and were not put to shame (vv. 4–5). Could this underlie the crowd's misunderstanding of Jesus' cry as his calling for Elijah? For illuminating interpretations of this psalm, see Ricoeur, "Lamentation as Prayer," 187–234. Bauckam's interpretation of Jesus' cry of dereliction in Mark underscores the reality of Jesus' godforsakenness. It was not an understandable mistake. Bauckam , however, does not push the consequences of Jesus being forsaken by God to the collapse of trust between Father and Son. "God's Self-Identification with the Godforsaken," 254–68.

The Self-Shaming God Who Reconciles

expected loyalty.[4] Clearly, the Father has given up the Son to godforsakenness.[5] Thus the utter dismay of the speakers of the psalms that we have cited in this book, along with the various voices in the Book of the Twelve who are shamed over experiencing God's withdrawal of promised loyalty, becomes concentrated in the Messiah who bore the terrible moment of God's giving up (cf. Isa 54:7).[6]

Congruent with the description of weariness in Ps 73 which attends unresolved understanding of theological shame, Luke portrays the inability of Jesus' follower to understand his messianic destiny of death and resurrection (Luke 18:32–34). Recalling the expectations voiced before his birth (Luke 2:68–74) and Jesus' own claims for his mission (Luke 4:18–19), Luke, alone among the gospels, describes how his followers recoil in shame under the impact of the Messiah's death. Jesus, by praying for the forgiveness of his executioners, throws into confusion the dream of national liberation to which his followers had been led to give their trust. The crowd who witnessed the entirety of his execution mourned and beat their breasts (Luke 23:27, 48). The men journeying to Emmaus stopped in their tracks "looking sad" when the unknown traveler asked them to repeat their discussion of the forfeiture of the Messiah to fulfill their hope of redeeming Israel (Luke 24:17, 21).[7]

The dynamic of the story immediately shifts from the shamed and confused disciples to Jesus who "beginning with Moses and all the prophets . . . interpreted to them the things about himself in all the scriptures (Was it not necessary that the Messiah should suffer these things and then enter into his glory? Luke 24:26–27). So, as in Ps 73 where the pull of the congregation draws the shamed and wearied one into the sanctuary for a reconfiguration of God and a rebirth of self, now Jesus reinterprets the image of Messiahship. Instead of a Messiah as earthly redeemer/liberator,

---

4. Wis 2:12–20 also may resonate here. See among many commentators Beare, *The Gospel according to Matthew*, 534 and Brown, *The Death of the Messiah*, 1043–51.

5. Hengel describes the shame of divine abandonment in *Crucifixion*. See the suggestive commentary on Matthew by Weber in *The Cross*, 114.

6. See Brueggemann, "A Shattered Transcendence," 169–82.

7. See John 16:20–22 where a harsh contrast is stuck between the shame of the disciples over their discredited messiah and the glee of the world that discredited him. For an exhaustive treatment of the Emmaus story see Dillon, *From Eye-Witnesses to Ministers of the Word*. Jones places this text in the existential moment of the traumatic events of 9/11 and brings out Jesus' re-framing of the disciples' trauma/shame in "Emmaus Witnessing," 125–28.

Living Beyond Shame within the Christian Canon

what comes to the forefront are images of the suffering, interceding servant whom God vindicates.[8] Jesus' reinterpretation is crucially validated through his revelatory eucharistic action (v. 30) and the disciples' registering their appropriation as their eyes being opened. "Were not our hearts burning within us while he was talking to us on the road, while he was opening the scriptures to us?" (v. 32).

Paul uses the psalms' language of shame to empower his message of the resurrection of the crucified messiah. Apostolic preaching on the resurrection carries forward the theme of reversal located in the psalms' message that God vindicates the suffering and the shamed by transferring to God's enemies the shame of those who experienced their plight as God's irrational forsakenness. "But God chose what is foolish in the world to shame the wise; God chose what is weak in the world to shame the strong; God chose what is low and despised in the world, things that are not, to reduce to nothing things that are" (1 Cor 1:27–28). The crucified Messiah is a scandal to Jews and folly to Greeks (Rom 9:33, 1 Cor 1:23, Gal 5:11), yet as the resurrected crucified Messiah, he is the stumbling block who shatters their assumptions.[9] This reversal of worldly values with its attendant transfer of shame bespeaks the eschatological upheaval of the ages that has been inaugurated by the crucifixion and resurrection of Jesus and his installation as continuing hope in believers. (Rom 5:5) This good news of the reversal of shame was preached through the widespread Christological appropriation of Isa 28:16 "Anyone who believes in him [Jesus] will not be put to shame"[10] (Rom 9:33, 10:11; 1 Pet 2:6).

---

8 See the work of Moessner, especially his "Good News for the 'Wilderness Generation,'" 1–34.

9. In Paul's discussion of life in the Christian community, to act as a stumbling block is to ridicule and undercut someone's position, to put someone to shame and cause that person to falter in faith. (1 Cor 8:13; Rom 14:13, 21; 2 Cor 11:29). For critical discussion see Conzelmann, *1 Corinthians*, 47.

10. Ibid., 50; and Käsemann, *Commentary on Romans*, 278–79. The NT is quoting the LXX. The Masoretic Text of Isa 28:16 reads יחיש "will hasten" (hiphil of חוש) which the Septuagint translates as καταισχυθῇ (be ashamed). The quotation may underlay the confessional statement in 2 Tim 1:12 "But I am not ashamed, for I know [in] whom I have put my trust, and I am sure that he is able to guard until that Day what I have entrusted to him." It is striking, indeed, that 2 Tim contains such a heavy concentration of issues of shame and trust, betrayal and loyalty as in 1:8, 15–16; 2:13, 15; 4:10–16. This is developed later in this chapter.

The Self-Shaming God Who Reconciles

A TRINITARIAN THEOLOGICAL CONSTRUCTION

With Jesus' cry of dereliction from the cross, shame enters the heavenly family of God. In the heart-breaking question, "Why have you forsaken me?" God the Son signals how abandonment by God the Father unleashed profound shame upon the Son of God. In the words of Alan E. Lewis, one of the most sensitive interpreters of this catastrophe of theological shame:

> [I]n the end all his claims of familiarity with God, directly spoken to "Abba" or obliquely hinted at, seemed hollow, incredible, and unspeakably ironic . . . Who is this man but a mere mortal, creaturely and finite, a fool or fraud at that, who, so convinced of the propinquity of God, dies aware only of God's abysmal, utter distance . . . For *him* to die abandoned and rejected, forsaken by the loving, heavenly Father to whose will he had sacrificed his all, surely meant wretchedness unlimited, shattering disillusionment, and hellishness unknown.[11]

Moreover, within the Trinitarian family of God the shame of the Son's abandonment redounds upon the self-shaming of God the Father. Lewis points out perceptively: "Is it then the *Father* who has proved a failure in the end, breaking faith with the Son who went from Gethsemane to Calvary staking everything on the filial certainty of heavenly companionship? . . . [N]ot that *he* [Jesus] has failed God in his death, but that in his death *God has failed him* . . . [T]hat by failing the Son, the Lord of all has failed the world and all who share the Son's humanity."[12]

The decision of God in advance to be shamed and to enter into self-shaming becomes the unique and indispensable beginning point of God's ultimate achievement of victory of God's Kingdom. This is the irreducible scandal of the New Testament's witness to the shamed God who saves.

However, as we have already noticed, in God's living with Israel God has already shown God's self vulnerable to being overcome by shame. Moses passionately intercedes for Israel in the wilderness. He argues that God's destruction of God's rebellious people will redound to God shaming God's self for not being able to accomplish God's intentions. This is effective in deterring the impending wrath (Exod 32:12; Num 14:16; Deut 9:28; Josh

---

11. Lewis, *Between Cross and Resurrection*, 52–54. Lewis builds has case in conversation with Karl Barth, Jürgen Moltmann, Eberhard Jüngel, and Hans Urs von Balthasar. See also the helpful treatment by Jinkins and Reid, "God's Forsakenness," 33–57.

12. Ibid., 54–55; see 192–93. Jinkins points out that this Trinitarian understanding of redemption is anticipated by Campbell in his *The Nature of Atonement*, 1856.

7:9). Israel's hectoring God in the laments has the intention of turning Israel's shame into a threat of impending shame to fall upon God for God's failure to live up to God's reputation if Israel is destroyed. Malachi reports the hurt Israel causes to God by their ridiculing God's ability to maintain justice. The Book of the Twelve is peppered with similar accusations against God. The striking metaphors of Isaiah's unfruitful vineyard, Hosea's incorrigible son, and Jeremiah's worthless loincloth make us aware of the pathos of shame that comes over God by being double-crossed by Israel. Isaiah 52–53 describe the paradoxical character of the Servant of the Lord who is exalted precisely because he poured out himself unto suffering, humiliation, and death.[13]

In the Gospels, the stories that lead up to the crucifixion foreshadow the impending shame of Golgotha. The gospel writers concentrate accounts of the shaming of God through the double-crossing of humans into the week between Jesus' triumphal entry and the crucifixion. Thus the parable of the wicked tenants (Matt 21:33–46 and parallels) has the owner of the vineyard sending his son in the misplaced confidence that the tenants will respect his son. Jesus weeps over Jerusalem because they would not respond to him like chicks do to the invitation of the mother hen to gather them under her wings (Matt 23:37–39 and parallels). The giver of the talents castigates the slothful servant for not having lived up to the master's expectation (Matt 25:14–30 and parallels). At the Last Supper Jesus applies the quotation from Zech 13:7 ("I will strike the shepherd and the sheep of the flock will be scattered") to the shattering of his disciples' trust under the impact of what is to happen to him (Matt 26:33 and parallels).[14] Jesus looks upon Peter after he has denied him three times (Luke 22:54–62 and parallels).

To summarize: Theological shame is the experience of God's failure to keep trust with one who trusts in God. What greater experience of that shame can there be than to what Jesus gave voice when he cried of being abandoned by God? (Matt 27:43–46). If trust between Father and Son is ripped apart on the cross, theological shame is brought into the bosom of the Godhead. God is self-shamed and self-shaming at Golgotha.[15]

13. See more on this in Bauckham, *God Crucified*, 58–61.

14. It is striking that Luke is the only gospel that does not retain this logion, perhaps because of his picture of Jesus as confident, suffering intercessor and the disciples' shame at the moment of crucifixion.

15. This theological position is heavily indebted to the discussion of the Trinity in Lewis, *Between Cross and Resurrection*, Part Two.

Yet, though the bonds of trust are being torn asunder as the betrayed one accuses God of a stunning failure, this accusation is caught up and held within the space of prayer, addressed to the very one who is called the betrayer. Noticing this, we become aware of the radical antithesis of unity within disunity in the Godhead between Father and Son, a tension that holds firm through the Spirit of love and unity, the third person of the Trinity. By God's drawing death into the heart of the Trinity, the Son suffers Godforsakenness and the Father suffers Sonlessness.

However, within the heart of the Trinity the Holy Spirit holds Father and Son together more powerfully than death can pull them apart. Under the power of the Spirit new life emerges out of death. Paul specifically points to the Spirit as the cause of the resurrection of Jesus (Rom 1:4 and 8:11). "It is God's own limitless abundance of possibility, the divine capacity to flourish and create new life by surrendering to nothingness and death, which grounds the possibility for perishable things to become new too. The victory over death which the resurrection promises us, as perishable creatures, depends wholly upon God's own creativity, which takes on the power of death, draws it into the divine life, and thereby overcomes it."[16]

In the midst of godforsakenness and godlessness, the heightening overflow of divine being in the resurrected Jesus outflanks sin, leaves hate exhausted, and secures the death of death, the negation of non-being.[17] The self-shamed and self-shaming God of Golgotha lives beyond shame and wins for the world's sake a way beyond shame. By virtue of the resurrection, the Father and the Son gain self-vindicating victory and life and hope for those who cry out for authentication.[18]

Thus the perpetrators of the death of God bear the final shame. "What a grotesque display of inept miscalculation, the boundlessness of human folly, the myopia of hatred!"[19]

---

16. Ibid., 247.
17. Ibid., 251 and 255.
18. Ibid., 97; see 61, 80, 87.
19. Ibid., 84; see 117, "Triumphant over the enemies of life, Jesus was now alive beside the Lord of life, sharing the divine glory, until he would come again, destroying every authority and power, that the Father might be all in all in the final reign of justice, peace, and love."

A NEW TESTAMENT PICTURE OF LIVING BEYOND SHAME

What might an attitude toward living look like from one who, while suffering shame, lives beyond it? The New Testament epistle of 2 Timothy suggests an answer to this question. This brief book contains possibly the clearest illustration of a Christian struggling with the shame of abandonment or near abandonment. The frankly personal statements of this letter writer open a window into the challenge of living through shame and beyond it.[20]

Before addressing the letter directly, however, attention must be paid to the canonical positioning of 2 Timothy. It is well known that this letter is part of a larger collection of letters commonly called the Pastorals all of which bear the name of the Apostle Paul as author. The critical questions attached to this authorial claim are well known and need no rehearsing here. What I will take seriously, though, is the fact that the Pastorals as they are ordered in the canon complete the collection of Paul's indubitably authentic letters and the deutero-Pauline letters. The Pastorals along with Romans form the "bookends" of the Pauline collection. Consequently, the Pastorals weigh heavily in the hermeneutical shaping of how the Pauline collection is to be received and used as Scripture.[21]

I begin by examining personal expressions of shame in the authentic letters of Paul. This will give us a perspective from which to assess 2 Timothy's treatment of personal shame. The dialogue between these positions will yield a "canonical Paul" whose example will serve Christians to discern a way for living beyond shame.

Shame first appears in a verbal expression in Rom 1:16 "For I am not ashamed (ἐπαισχύνομαι) of the gospel." This in itself is significant since Romans together with the Pastorals form the bookends of the Pauline corpus. It is striking that shame shows up very quickly in Romans, the book that systematically surveys the different theological points of Paul's particular letters as an introduction to the Pauline collection, and in 2 Timothy, the book that presents itself as Paul's valedictory statement.[22] The context of the

---

20. The question of authorship of the Pastoral Epistles poses a perennial debate among scholars. For an introduction to the issues and a suggestion of a way to appreciate the Pauline character of the pastorals, see the commentary of Dunn, *The New Interpreter's Bible*. See also the helpful commentary by Johnson, *The First and Second Letters to Timothy*..

21. For a convenient summary of the arguments that support this hermeneutical role of the Pastorals see Childs, *The Church's Guide for Reading Paul*, 70–76.

22. Titus is principally concerned with communicating patterns of behavior for the church.

citation in Romans indicates that the issue of shame relates to the question of the gospel's power. Paul's assertion that he is not ashamed amounts to a confessional statement expressed negatively. The sense of the assertion is that the gospel is not powerless in the world. "It is God's declaration of salvation to the world, which is outside human control . . . and which constantly becomes a reality itself in proclamation in the power of the Spirit."[23] Because of the divine origin of the gospel Paul may be confident, that is, he need not be ashamed that the gospel will disappoint him.[24] Already in the opening verses of Romans we are met with the notion of the trust God provides which is critical to the human witness to the gospel.

Paul struggles with shame as a personal issue in the letter to the Philippians. The setting of this letter is a prison experience. Paul's "eager expectation and hope" (1:20) is that the suffering of his imprisonment will not put him to shame in any way. The shame Paul hopes to avoid is the shame of cowardice. Paul does not want his imprisonment to silence him. In the situation of imprisonment Paul, and by extension his co-workers, feel the coercive power of the state exacerbated by the opposition of those who "proclaim Christ from envy . . . intending to increase my suffering" (1:15, 17). This creates a crisis of remaining firm in commitment to the gospel. The shame Paul wishes to avoid, even at the cost of life, is the abandonment of faithfulness to the gospel.

This goal of not abandoning, of standing firm in one spirit (1:27–28), becomes a major sub-text for the Epistle to the Philippians. Paul wishes to continue to speak boldly, and he claims that the sharing in Christ's sufferings and the power of his resurrection (3:10) provides him with the confidence that he will continue to witness to Christ in his imprisonment. Indeed, he rejoices that by his example other Christians persevere in their witness "with greater boldness and without fear" (1:14, see also 1:28).

No where does Paul indicate that his suffering and imprisonment for the sake of the gospel causes him shame. This is surprising, given the conventional notions of shame in his world. "Nothing could be more shameful in the eyes of the world than the death by execution that Jesus had undergone, or the suffering of contempt and rejection experienced by those who gathered in his name and proclaimed him as their Lord."[25] I believe that

---

23. Käsemann, *Commentary on Romans*, 22.

24. See the insightful comments on the Christian's stance with the gospel before the world by Barth, *The Epistle to the Romans*, 35.

25 Johnson, *The First and Second Letters to Timothy*, 358.

Paul's eschatological orientation prevents him from abandoning the gospel to his own shame. His union with Christ crucified and raised from the dead (3:10–11) has neutralized conventional notions of shame, notions which the state apparatus and competing proclaimers in the Philippian church are trying to use to their advantage.[26]

Looking at Romans and Philippians together, those who are engaged in missionary activity must contend with shame. While the gospel proclaims that the one who is Lord was crucified, God has made the gospel a thing of power so that the one who proclaims it need not be made to feel ashamed of confessing to something weak. Conversely, when, for the sake of the gospel, the evangelist is subjected to intimidation, the gospel itself provides power so that the evangelist will not to be put to shame by abandoning that gospel. The gospel will not default on expectations so that one would be ashamed of the gospel (Romans), and the gospel's power will not permit one to default on the gospel's expectations in the face of intimidation so that one would be ashamed of oneself (Philippians). From this position we can consider 2 Timothy.

The writer of 2 Timothy has suffered near-abandonment. He calls himself Paul, though significant reasons weigh against identifying this person with the apostle Paul. Nonetheless, the canon has linked this letter with the genuine letters of Paul as the completion of the Pauline corpus.

Suffering, in prison and anticipating execution Paul writes that at his first defense "no one came to my support, but all deserted me. May it not be counted against them! But the Lord stood by me and gave me strength." (4:16–17) The rhetoric of the letter is a reflex of this experience of near-abandonment with the purpose of invigorating its timid addressee, Timothy.[27] "Do your best to come to me soon . . . Get Mark and bring him with you" (4:9, 11). "Do your best to come before winter" (4:21).

The ignoble character of Jesus' death coupled with the shame of imprisonment produces shocking and debilitating effects upon his followers. Again, conventional notions of shame threaten the substance of the gospel to goad the believer's abandonment of it.[28] Paul's experience of

---

26. See the perceptive comments by Markus Barth, *Ephesians*, 359–62. On Paul regarding himself as an eschatologic person, see Fridrichsen, "The Apostle and His Message," 232–50.

27. Johnson, "II Timothy," 6.

28. Hebrews 10:32–35 describes the shame inducing effects of imprisonment: prisoners are abandoned by friends when publically exposed; in the face of having one's possessions plundered the victim abandons the confidence that "you yourselves possessed something better and more lasting."

The Self-Shaming God Who Reconciles

abandonment by trusted friends is searing and vivid. "You are aware that all who are in Asia have turned away from me, including Phygelus and Hermogenes" (1:15). "Demus, in love with this present world, has deserted me . . . Alexander the coppersmith did me great harm . . . You also must beware of him" (4:9,14). "Hymenaeus and Philetus, who have swerved from the truth" (2:17–18). The prisoner is deprived and has need of books, parchments and a cloak (4:13).

Against this backdrop of cascading abandonment, a precious few have withstood the threat of shame and proved faithful. "Onesiphorus . . . often refreshed me and was not ashamed of my chains; when he arrived in Rome, he eagerly searched for me and found me" (1:16–17). "Only Luke is with me" (4:11). "The Lord stood by me and gave me strength" (4:17).

It is the gospel for which Paul is "suffering and wearing fetters like a criminal" (2:9). The gospel is the proclamation that Jesus as Savior has abolished the power of death and has brought life and immortality to light (1:10).[29] This proclamation strikes at the heart of the power of the state, since the abolishment of death and the revelation of life and immortality are aimed to neutralize the state's penalties to coerce compliance with authority through the threat of suffering, imprisonment, abandonment and impending death. Specifically Paul is afraid that Timothy will be swept away in the rush to the exits by erstwhile supporters who have become intimidated.[30] He pleads with Timothy to remember his upbringing in the faith and to rekindle this gift of faith "for God did not give us a spirit of timidity but a spirit of power and love and self-control" (1:7). Timothy must not become a coward.[31]

Paul employs a wide array of rhetorical strategies to encourage Timothy. Some of these are: analogies (2:3–6), preformed testimonies (2:8, 11–13, 19; 3:16), pedagogy and coaching (2:16, 20–26), and forecasting

---

29. The attribution of the title Savior to Jesus is rare in the genuine letters of Paul, found only in Phil 3:20 where the title is used to denominate Jesus in his role of transformer at the parousia. The designation of Jesus as Savior confronted the language of the Hellenistic mystery religions as well as the cult of the emperor. See Dibelius and Conzelmann, *The Pastoral Epistles*, 101–3.

30. In Heb 10:32–39 the addressees are praised that they did not "shrink back" and did not abandon the confidence that "you yourselves possessed something better and more lasting" in the face of having one's possessions plundered. This is the context for the classic definition of faith in Heb 11:1 "Now faith is the assurance of things hoped for, the conviction of things not seen."

31. First Corinthians 16:10–11 contains insights that suggest Timothy's need for reassurance.

end-time behavior (3:1–9). But the strongest encouragement comes from Paul's personal testimony where he confronts directly the issue of shame.[32]

Frankly admitting that his appointment as preacher, apostle and teacher of the gospel has brought the suffering of a criminal upon him (1:11), Paul states emphatically "But I am not ashamed" (1:12). The context of criminal suffering with the intent of coercing Paul's silence suggests that the shame Paul is denying is that of cowardice. Paul backs up his defiant denial by continuing his personal testimony "for I know whom I have believed, and I am sure that he is able to guard until that Day what has been entrusted to me." This confessional statement shows signs of being crafted after careful reflection. Paul's appointment (ἐτέθην) to the gospel will not be broken through the shame of cowardice, for the one in whom Paul places his trust will guard that which has been appointed to (παραθήκην) Paul. Paul's appointment sets up expectations that Paul will meet. Paul's placement of trust in Jesus Savior sets up expectations that Paul knows Jesus will keep.

The pivot in this reciprocal relationship is the personal knowledge Paul confesses of the one in whom he has put his trust and of the power of Jesus Savior to keep safely Paul's appointment, both the carrying out of his office and the content of the gospel. The importance Paul gives to this personal testimony is indicated by its framing the entire letter. It appears in 2 Tim 1 before any other of the rhetorical strategies Paul uses to engage Timothy. In 2 Tim 4 the final words of the epistle which precede the greetings assert again this personal knowledge of the one in whom Paul has put his trust to guard his appointment. "But the Lord stood by me and gave me strength to proclaim the word fully, that all the Gentiles might hear it. So I was rescued from the lion's mouth.[33] The Lord will rescue me from every evil and save me for his heavenly kingdom" (4:17–18).

In between these framing testimonies, Paul inserts a brief résumé of his apostolic travails with a clear directive to Timothy to take courage from

---

32. Johnson, "II Timothy," 7. The relationship of mentor to protégé (Phil 2:22) accounts for the weight given to personal testimony.

33. The reference of being saved from the lion's mouth is striking. Is the referent Daniel abandoned to the lion's den? More specifically might be the Septuagint's translation of Ps 22:21 Σῶσον με ἐκ στόματο λέοντος "save me from the mouth of the lion" (LXX 21.21). The occurrence of this phrase from this psalm whose opening lines formed Jesus' cry of abandonment from the Cross underscores how the possibility of caving in (shame) was such a profound threat and how a deep trust in the Savior became critical to living beyond this threat.

The Self-Shaming God Who Reconciles

his example: "Now you have observed my teaching, my conduct, my aim in life, my faith, my patience, my love, my steadfastness, my persecutions, my sufferings, what befell me at Antioch, at Iconium, and at Lystra, what persecutions I endured; yet from them all the Lord rescued me. Indeed all who desire to live a godly life in Christ Jesus will be persecuted... But as for you, continue in what you have learned and have firmly believed" (3:10-12, 14).

Certainly Paul intends his personal testimony to be the most telling of all rhetorical strategies in stiffening Timothy's resolve.[34] "Follow the pattern of the sound words which you have heard from me, in the faith and love which are in Christ Jesus; guard the truth that has been entrusted to you by the Holy Spirit who dwells within us" (1:13). As the gospel was entrusted to Paul, so the truth has been entrusted to Timothy.[35] To a degree, the entrustment of that next generation to Timothy happens through Timothy's following the example of Paul. This is the basis for his command, "Do not be ashamed then of testifying to our Lord, nor of me his prisoner, but take your share of suffering for the gospel in the power of God" (1:8) and "Take your share of suffering as a good soldier of Christ Jesus" (2:3). "Do your best to present yourself to God as one approved, a workman who has no need to be ashamed" (2:15).[36]

In sum, the writer of 2 Timothy knows the shame of experiencing presumed trusted colleagues abandoning him because his situation was

---

34. Note the striking parallels between Paul's valedictory words and the farewell address to the elders of the church in Ephesus in Acts 20:18-35. Paul submits that in the midst of trials he did not shrink back (vv. 20, 27), that he only wishes to accomplish his course (v. 24), that he has lived an exemplary life (v.33), and that he is entrusting to them the work he will no longer be present to do (v. 28-32). The similarity has posed the question whether 2 Timothy is in the form of a farewell discourse like those found in the Old Testament and other ancient Jewish literature. For adoption of this view see Tannehill, *The Narrative Unity of Luke-Acts, II,* 252, and Conzelmann, *Acts of the Apostles,* 173. However, Johnson, *The First and Second Letters to Timothy,* 322, asserts "that another literary genre fits its literary self-presentation better: the personal paraenetic letter."

35. This passing of the good news from mentor to protégé is decisive in choosing "what has been entrusted to me" over "what I have entrusted to him" as the translation of τὴν παραθήκαν μου (1:12). This text has been cited by Käsemann as an indicator of early tendencies toward catholicism, but this has been disputed by subsequent research from German Roman Catholic scholars, especially Gerhard Lohfink. See Childs, *The Church's Guide for Reading Paul,* 70-76.

36. See Aageson, "The Pastoral Epistles," 15: "the text of the epistle personifies the link representing and conveying the apostle, his theology, and suffering to the recipients of 2 Timothy in the hope that they will follow his example and be united with him in this act of suffering."

intimidating. Nevertheless, he perseveres in living beyond shame. He claims the power of the good news that Jesus Savior has conquered death and revealed life and immortality to him. He clings to personal knowledge of the presence of his Savior in his abandonment. He carries on in fighting the good fight, finishing the race and keeping the faith. His example teaches his readers to have similar stamina. [37]

Taken together, the texts in the Pauline canon which reflect the struggle against shame yield a compelling composite of living beyond shame. Indispensible is the superior power of God manifested through the gospel which is centered on the victory God has won through Christ over death and the subsequent opening up of new life. This gospel is both a gift of a new way of orienting one's life and a calling to be faithful to the giver of this gift.

Drawing upon the tableaux within the Book of the Twelve, reflected upon in Pss 73–75, and 2 Timothy, a composite picture of living beyond shame begins to emerge. This picture reflects a frank recognition of forces that would seek to nullify the gospel's gift of trust and supplant God's sovereignty. It does not belittle the ability of such forces to intimidate and to coerce silence, and it acknowledges the struggles of abandonment and despair. Yet, this picture of living beyond shame vividly disputes such negativity with an engaging illustration of warm, personal, living faithfulness in the presence of the Lord especially when one is in the throes of abandonment. That one can be so oriented under such conditions is only possible because the Lord has determined not to be put to shame, but to overcome it. The perseverance which is the outcome of this divine presence is an example which inspires hope and courage among those who have eyes to see.

---

37. Johnson draws the parallels between the abandonment of Paul and its potential for producing shame, on the one hand, and Timothy's future experience of abandonment: "Now we see that Timothy must face abandonment, when men do not wish to listen to his words, but follow after false teachers (3:1, 4:3). He will face abandonment just as the Apostle. In the face of this, Timothy is to willingly take part in the suffering, to persevere in his work of preaching and teaching, not filled with cowardice (1:7) or shame (1:8, 3:15), but empowered with that Spirit who is able to sustain him through suffering and rejection (1:8; 2:1) just as He had Paul (1:12)."

5

The Self-Shamed God Who Reconciles
A Contribution to Pastoral Theology and Practice

SUMMARY OF THE DISCUSSION

The type of shame under consideration pertains to a state of being, an orientation to existence, which is bound up with a relationship of trust that has failed. To be put to shame, as the Bible frequently describes this state of being, is to suffer the breakdown of a trusting relationship. The evidence of this breakdown usually points to one party in the relationship failing to live up to the terms of the relationship as understood by the shamed party. In chapter 2 we noticed instances in the Old Testament where this occurs in human relationships. Our principle concern, though, is studying situations where God is called out as the one who fails to be faithful. Perhaps it is not too far off the mark to call this "believer's shame."

Psalm 22:5 epitomizes a recurring refrain: "In you they trusted and were not put to shame." Speakers in the Psalms worry about experiencing the breakdown of the trusting relationship with God at the point where God's promises, specifically the "two ways" formula of life (Ps 1:6), fail to actualize in their lives. When something happens in the speaker's world to signal a forfeiture of God's promises, God is called out as the one who has put the speaker to shame.[1] By denominating God as the shamer, psalm

---

1. Third parties may contribute to this state of shame by capitalizing on the vulnerability of the person put to shame. Thus Jeremiah, after describing in most violent terms his experience of being cast into shame by God ("O Lord, you have raped me, and I was raped," 20:7), continues his lament by laying out the campaign of denigration prosecuted by his enemies which his state of shame has encouraged (20:10). For critical discussion of this passage see fn. 17.

speakers do more than protest with utter candor against the violation of trust. They also lay the groundwork for putting God to shame by placing God's trustworthiness in jeopardy. This seems to be the intent of the hectoring and commanding speech of protest (e.g., Ps 74:12–19).[2]

Clearly "believer's shame" is incompatible with the claims of divine sovereignty, particularly as that sovereignty underwrites the validity of the "two ways" formula. Therefore, the way God resolves this threat and restores the integrity of God's intentions participates in God's work of righteousness and grace. The Psalms typically show God making whole again the relationship with the shamed believer with the redounding of shame upon the agent or agents whose actions precipitated believer's shame. Ultimately, the hope is that this judgment will compel the shamer's humble acknowledgement of God's sovereignty and thus lay the basis for reconciliation to God and with the community of believers.

The Psalms graphically demonstrate that someone who is put to shame will be beset with one or more of a variety of affections. A partial list would include embarrassment, anger, a feeling of unworthiness and being soiled, violated, exploited, abandoned, bewildered. These affections are not shame itself but are rooted in a more primal state of experiencing the breakdown of a trusting relationship.

The triumphant word of the gospel, witnessed to by both testaments, is that God takes the side of those who suffer when bonds of trust are violated. As we have seen in chapters 2 and 4, both the psalmists and Paul use the language of the transfer of shame from the shamee to the shamer to describe what happens when God takes the side of the shamed. This divine response to shame has profound consequences when God is exposed as the shamer. We will explore those consequences in the ensuing discussion. Both the psalmists and Paul also employ the language of praise or boasting to mark the release of shame's hold upon the shamee.

In chapter 4 when we placed our biblical findings in conversation with modern theologians in the Reformed tradition, we were led to a deepening probing of the Trinitarian fracturing of God in the story of the passion of Jesus Christ. Theological shame is the experience of God's failure to keep trust with one who trusts in God. What greater experience of that shame can there be than to what Jesus gave voice when he cried of being

---

2. See Exod 32:11–14 for a similar instance where Moses pleads with God to consider how God's reputation will be embarrassed if God abandons the idolatrous Israelites in the wilderness.

abandoned by God (Matt 27:43–46)? If trust between Father and Son is ripped apart on the cross, theological shame is brought into the bosom of the Godhead. God is self-shamed at Golgotha.[3]

Thus it is only by virtue of the Spirit's raising the dead Jesus from the grave that trust is restored between Father and Son and the powers of this world are put to shame. Jesus resurrected now lives and rules beyond shame's reach. It is upon this basis that the good news can be preached to the world, "The one who trusts in Jesus will not be put to shame" (Rom 9:33; 10:11; 1 Pet 2:6; 3:16). The Book of the Twelve and 2 Timothy provide examples of living by that trust in conditions that create shame.

A CONTRIBUTION TO PASTORAL THEOLOGY[4]

The gospel's promise aims at two experiences of a state of shame that are brought about by a failed risk of trust. However discrete, these two centers of experienced shame are intimately connected because both share in common the understanding of life as lived in relationship. As humans we risk trusting ourselves to each other. When our partner in trust abrogates that trust in any way, we experience the collection of feelings we are calling shame: embarrassment, feeling unworthy or soiled, anger at ourselves and others for not defending against being taken advantage of, uncertainty about our ability for good judgment, fear of risking trust anew, to name the most common.

But this experience is not confined to our human interactions, and here is where we meet the second center of felt shame. Human shame may also bleed over into sensing that God has played falsely with us, and the same collection of feelings may color our thinking about God.[5]

Dorothee Sölle in her searching examination of suffering describes this link between the breakdown of trust and Godforsakenness: "Every suffering that is experienced as a threat to one's own life touches our relationship to God, if we use this expression in the strict theological sense. That

---

3. This theological position is heavily indebted to the discussion of the Trinity in Lewis, *Between Cross and Resurrection*, Part Two.

4. For a recent survey and analysis of pastoral theological methodologies see Park, "An Evolving History and Methodology," 5–33. This study has affinities with the Pastoral Reflection Method in Park's analysis.

5. See Ramsay, "Confronting Family Violence"; and Fortune, *Is Nothing Sacred?* chapter 5. Fortune describes graphically the shame that comes over the victim of clergy sexual abuse.

is, if we don't think of it as an attribute that some people have, like musical ability, but as something everyone possess, as that 'which a person trusts' (Luther). This (nonexplicit) relationship to God is called into question in extreme suffering. The ground on which life was built, the primal trust in the world's reliability—a reliability conveyed in many diverse ways—is destroyed."[6]

Examples abound. One spouse betrays another. A child is battered or exploited by a parent or relative. A woman is date-raped. A gay, lesbian, bi-sexual or transgendered person is "outed" in a humiliating way. A parent is repudiated by a child. A child is abandoned by a parent. An employee embezzles his employer. A pensioner is defrauded her pension. A parishioner is taken advantage of by her minister. An older worker is fired shortly before becoming eligible for retirement benefits. A veteran is denied his medical benefits. It is but a short step for many to think that God has played them falsely as well. Conversely, an experience that leads us to believe that God has played falsely with us may condition other human relationships that presuppose trust.

As pastors, we are called to stand with those shamed and witness to the Word of the self-shaming God who rises above shame. There is no greater experience of shame than that which convulsed the Trinity. We say this, however, not to trivialize instances of human shame, but to show that God stands in close solidarity with those so shamed. As pastors we are commissioned to say, "You are not alone in the degradation of your shame. You have a friend in the shamed Jesus who suffered the shame of abandonment by his disciples and his God."

Yet, this solidarity in shame is but the necessary foundation for the pastor's witness to the Spirit's restoration of trust between Son and Father in the resurrection of Jesus and the power that restoration has for renewing in ourselves inclinations to trust that have been shattered. Within the context of solidarity between the shamed human and the self-shamed God who lives beyond shame, the Spirit speaks the word in us that kindles renewed trust. Only from inside the broken relationship of trust can God speak into the condition of broken trust the power to heal, to restore faith in God and in ourselves.[7] Standing with those shamed as a witness to the shamed

---

6. *Suffering*, 86.

7. Hooker, "Interchange in Christ," 349–61, and "Interchange in Christ and Ethics," 3–17. Jinkins and Reid provide a useful survey of patristic and Reformed theological witness to God's assumption of our shame in order that God may heal us. "God's Forsakenness," 45–47.

The Self-Shaming God Who Reconciles

God who lives beyond shame, the pastor prays for the Spirit to bring about restoration of trust, and in trusting ways the pastor models new relations with women, men and children who have suffered horribly the ravages of broken promises.[8]

Pastors will need to adopt an eclectic approach in ministering to shamed persons. Herman's experience in treating persons with Post Traumatic Stress Syndrome underlines how critical it is to establish a context of safety for the traumatized wherein the story of trauma can be reconstructed.[9] This resonates with the theological requirement of situating the story of shame within the self-shaming God. The sharing of shame within the story of the self-shaming God is akin to externalizing shame, a suggestion offered by McNish[10] and Albers,[11] and can be facilitated by the use of a 12-step program. Capps' insight into the power of mirroring between therapist and patient as constitutive of healing offers another way for pastors to access the theological power of shared shame between the shamed and God.[12] In her exegesis of Pss 22–23, Ramsay sets out crucial criteria for preaching to victims of shame.[13]

To summarize, there is good news for the shamed. God knows your plight in the shame of the Son abandoned on the cross. Jesus' resurrection demonstrates the power of the Spirit to open the way for you to live beyond shame.[14]

---

8. See the helpful use of Ps 23 in pastoral care of broken relationships of trust in Ramsay, "Compassionate Resistance," 217–26.

9. Herman, *Trauma and Recovery*, 3.

10. McNish, *Transforming Shame*, 190–94.

11. Albers, *Shame: A Faith Perspective*, 132.

12. Capps, *The Depleted Self*, 91. Capps construes mirroring as "self-mirroring" whereas I have appropriated the concept as an apt way of describing the relationship between the shamed and God that the pastor mediates.

13. Ramsay, "Preaching to Survivors of Child Sexual Abuse," 58–70. In her exegesis of Ps 22, Ramsay underscores the importance of this psalm in the narratives of Jesus passion and the powerful implications this has for ministry with shamed persons. However, her interpretation of the meaning of the cross centers on resistance to violence rather than succumbing to it in order to overcome it. "Incarnation occurs not so that Jesus might suffer abuse but so that we might see the power of love to actively resist forces that destroy and deform human life. Here, the cross becomes a symbol of God's active, determined resistance to evil and triumph over it. Obviously evil is not utterly defeated, but the larger power of compassionate love is demonstrated convincingly." 67. This theological position in my judgment does not go far enough in demonstrating divine solidarity with the shamed person.

14. See Moltmann's use of Hegel's phrase, "seizing death," to describe life beyond shame in "The 'Crucified God,'" 36–37. "Whenever men [sic] suffer because they love,

But what about the shamers? What about the fate of those who despitefully use you? What about those who crucified Jesus? Have we exhausted our pastoral witness when we say that God has transferred the shame they caused upon their heads? Is there nothing more to say? Is there no possibility for reconciliation between shamer and shamee?

Certainly, the resurrection does "shame the strong" (1 Cor 1:27–28). The resurrection demonstrates to the strong the failure of convictions upon which they risked everything, covering them now with shame.[15]

However this dividing up the world between the shamed and the saved is not the final word of the gospel. There is a universal thrust to the gospel's claim that the entire world will know the God who reigns in love and justice (Isa 2; Col 1:15–20). The question becomes critical: What might move the newly shamed to reconciliation with the God who has now shamed them and to reconciliation with those they had previously put to shame?

This question can be approached from the opposite direction, as well. The people of God are commanded not to hold vengeance, to pray for enemies, and to forgive as they have been forgiven (Rom 12:14–21; Matt 5:43–48). What possibly could persuade those who have suffered the ravages of being despitefully used to be reconciled with those who despitefully used them and now are saddled with the shame of judgment?

Again, we must search for a starting point outside the fractured human relationship and within the fractured Trinitarian understanding of God. This time we recall that in the cry of dereliction from the cross, Jesus identifies his Father as the one who has abandoned him and put him to shame. The Father is the shamer of the Son.[16] God is the self-shamer and makes company with everyone who despitefully uses whomever enters into a relationship of trust.[17] The one who is responsible for executing judgment

---

God suffers with them. God suffered Jesus' death and proved the strength of his love in that suffering. This same suffering enables men [sic] to find the strength to endure what threatens to annihilate them, and to 'seize death'. Hegel called this seizing death 'the life of the spirit, which is not a life that recoils from death and protects itself from devastation, but a life which endures death and preserves itself in it.' (*Phänomenologie des Geistes, Werke* [ed. Gockner], 2, 34)."

15. No more horrifying description of the shaming of the strong can be found than Rev 18.

16. In Luke Jesus is portrayed as being the instigator of shame in the disciples by forfeiting his Messianic claim as liberator through the act of praying for his executioners on the cross. See chapter 4.

17. In an astonishing turn of phrase Jeremiah accuses God of "raping" him as the way of expressing his feeling of God's breaking trust with him (Jer 20:7–10, 18) see

The Self-Shaming God Who Reconciles

upon shamers is the very one who causes shame and thereby shares in the judgment of the shamer. What better proof can there be that the God who transfers shame in judgment wants to come close and take the side of those so judged? (Isa 53:9; Luke 19:1–10; John 8:1–11). Is this not the first step God takes in reconciling shamers to God?[18]

Here, in the company of the self-shaming God, those who bear the judgment of trampling upon trust may hear the Spirit calling again Father and Son to renewed relationship of trust in the resurrection of Jesus. They may hear that same word from the Spirit calling everyone to the opportunity to repent from despiteful practices and to embark upon the ways of trust. Because the self-shaming God draws near to those judged, the restored Trinity can invite the judged ones into a new community (2 Cor 5:16–21; Rom 5:6–10).[19]

Thus the eschatological role of the Spirit, making room for the reclaiming of the shamer, marks a fundamental qualification of the two-ways formula, even as that formula is affirmed. The self-shaming God aligns with the wicked in their shame and perishes with the wicked so that even the wicked may become righteous as the Spirit calls the Father and the Son back to life.

Pastors are commissioned to the difficult task of hearing and authenticating situations and conditions that convey a judgment of those who have exploited persons who reposed their trust in them. But in solidarity with

---

Brueggemann, *A Commentary on Jeremiah*, 181; and Stulman, "Jeremiah as a Polyphonic Response to Suffering," 309–11. For interpretations that uphold the motif of deception without sexual overtones, see Smith, *The Laments of Jeremiah*, 24; and O'Connor, *The Confessions of Jeremiah*, 70–71.

18. This position is not articulated with sufficient precision in treatments of the crucifixion. For example, Jinkins and Reid, "God's Forsakenness," 42–43 argue that "the Father, in his necessary and utter leave-taking of the Son, will not forsake the Son utterly. The Father stands over-against the Son in the most terrible opposition; yet the Father is bound to the Son in divine love." Maintaining this position not only diminishes the full impact of the three-day disintegration in the grave, but also undercuts the pastoral impact of God's assuming, in the person of the Father, the fate of those who put others to shame. More to the point of our argument is the observation of Moltmann, "God's Forsakenness," 29, 33: "Jesus' death means that not only God's faithfulness, but also the very deity of God, whose closeness and fatherhood Jesus had proclaimed, are at stake . . . In the Pauline view, Jesus suffered death abandoned by God, the Father. The Father, on the other hand, suffered the death of his Son in the pain of his love." See this same article for Moltmann's explanation of how this position does not incur the charge of patripassianism.

19. See Keck, "Justification of the Ungodly and Ethics," 199–209.

The Self-Shamed God Who Reconciles

those judged, they are commanded to witness to the God who joins the judged in judgment and who speaks the word of new beginning. Pastors will invite those judged to trust God's invitation of a new beginning. Pastors will make themselves available to hear confession, to grant absolution and to counsel in planning a pathway of penitence.

In reporting on his work with violent men, Livingston offers a model for the pastoral care of the shamers that draws upon the classical theology of Thomas Aquinas.[20] Livingston found that guiding offenders through the steps of Contrition through Confession and Satisfaction before reaching Absolution offered a genuine possibility of containing violent behavior. The steps that Livingston charts provide a ready access to the power that is available within the solidarity of the self-shaming God and shamers.[21]

In other words, the identification of the self-shaming God with the judgment of the shamers offers the opportunity to re-frame who the judged will be from now on.[22] This re-framing provides an opportunity for reconciliation between the person shamed and the shamer. The memory of the exploitation and its envelope of shame will not, indeed must not, be

---

20. Livingston, *Healing Violent Men,* 23, 69–80.

21. For preaching to perpetrators, Poling lays out important guidelines for exegesis that involve reformulation of doctrines of patriarchy. Less helpful are his suggestions on the restorative care of perpetrators. See his "Preaching to Perpetrators of Violence," 71–82.

22. See the pastoral guidance congruent with position we have been developing offered by Lewis, "Therefore the three-day gospel story at the center of our faith gives pastors words to speak of God's peace and forgiveness for those who face death with guilt and fear; and words of liberation for those in bondage to disease and pain. But it also impels them to act on behalf of all who are outraged at life's injustices and death's indignities. All sorts of little deeds, from personal gestures of understanding to the provision of group support, may aptly respond to the bewilderment, belligerence or bitterness we may encounter in the dying or the mourning. Yet what, finally and realistically, can be said and done when everyone involved feels so impotent and tongue-tied before tragedy, grief and suffering? Little that is meaningful, this author can testify, as both victim and perpetrator of gross, sometimes hilarious, pastoral ineptitude! Little, that is, beyond a Christlike, cruciform togetherness which weeps with those who weep and rages with those who rage. But perhaps when we do merely that, we do everything. Only by sitting beside the indignant could we hope to edge some of them towards the moment of disclosure when they understand that God is not the proper target of their fury, but their companion in it. If we allow our words, our manner, our status or professionalism, or—deadliest of all in certain circumstances—our breezy faith and heroic confidence, to distance us from those who doubt and stumble, weep and hurt, we surely betray the God of the cross and of the grave, obscuring the truth that their vexation is but a shadow of God's own anger, and their tears an earthly drop in the ocean of heavenly grief." "The Theology of Death and the Care of the Dying," 13. On re-framing, see Jones, "Emmaus Witnessing," 120.

The Self-Shaming God Who Reconciles

forgotten. But the memory loses its power to paralyze movement toward healing and ultimately destroy both shamer and the person shamed. In some cases relationships may be restored on different footings. In other cases relationships may be brought to a close with permission and empowerment of shamer and shamee to embark on different ones, now both chastened and wiser.[23] In all events, everyone is dependent upon the God who draws shame into the bosom of the divine family and lets it do its worst so that God can win for the world's sake a way beyond shame and offer that way as a gift of grace.

The Congregational Setting of the Pastoral Care of the Shamed

The pastoral care of the shamed addresses issues that are best approached in an individual or small group setting. Yet, our investigation of the biblical evidence has uncovered a strong emphasis upon the communal context of the effects of an outbreak of theological shame and the community's response to that outbreak. We saw in the Book of the Twelve a three-pronged community response to shame: continued confrontation with the raw facts of shame experienced as God's reneging on God's promises, the intense struggle of befuddled believers to regain commitment, and God's promise to uphold the validity of the two ways. Psalms 73–74 give this community response further reflection and expansion.

Both Pss 73–74 describe the breakdown of community under the pressure of the evidence of theological shame. In Ps 73 the prosperous wicked deal in pride and violence. They scoff and speak with malice, threatening high-handed oppression. That they feel secure in this strutting behavior is made plain in their mocking of God's impotence: "How can God know? Is there knowledge in the Most High?" (v. 11). The consequence of such arrogance is that "they [the wicked] pound His people again and again, until they are drained of their very last tear"(v. 10).[24] The ability of the wicked to wax prosperous by wreaking unchecked havoc in the community destroys not only the fabric of the community but more acutely, the integrity and constancy of the two-ways formula of life on which community is founded.

---

23. See the helpful comments of Livingston in the Introduction above, 11–12, and Smedes, *Shame and Grace*, 136.

24. It is impossible for v. 10 to yield a clear translation from the MT because of textual corruption. The one adopted here is found in the Jewish Publication Society's *Tanakh— The Holy Scriptures*.

This contributes to the depth of theological shame of the psalms speaker who has risked living by that formula.

In Ps 74:20–21, concomitant with the shame-producing destruction of the dwelling place of God, the poor, downtrodden and needy are violated. In this context of violence shame erupts as the psalmist's trust in God proves ill-founded. It is notable that the protest against God is expressed through the psalmist's commitment to community. "Remember thy congregation" (v. 2) and "Have regard for your covenant" (v. 20) underscore the threat that theological shame directs against the life of the community.

Members of any community of believers can testify to how the shame that overcomes a believer bleeds into damaging the health of the believing community.[25] When one spouse betrays another, a child is battered or exploited, a woman is date-raped, a gay, lesbian, bi-sexual or transgendered person is humiliated, a parent is repudiated by a child, a parent abandons a child, an employee embezzles the company, a pensioner is defrauded her pension, an older worker is fired in order to deny full benefits, or a veteran's claim is turned down, the effect is to chill all relationships that are founded on trust. Particularly is this acute when a trusted leader exploits the trust within an unequal power relationship. The petition of Ps 69:6 acknowledges how what happens to one person may threaten the community's spiritual health.

> Let not those who hope in thee be put to shame through me . . .
> Let not those who seek thee be brought to dishonor through me.

This setting of pastoral response to theological shame within the community throws light upon a dual responsibility of pastors. Congruent with the action of the saving-judging God (Ps 75:2–5) they are to preserve the health of the community through taking the initiative to work vigilantly for justice, to model trust in their dealings with congregants, and to create a congregational culture that honors trusting relationships.

But when shame erupts, pastors will function aggressively in their community to care for it and return it to health. In the latter case pastors and church leaders will confidently build their healing ministry upon the theology of the self-shamed God who reconciles. Obedient to this theology, pastors will reach out to both the shamed and the perpetrator. This

---

25. See, Jones, "Emmaus Witnessing," 117: "To many, the collateral damage of such violence is not as immediately evident as is the damage to the more easily identified victims; and because of this, the traces it leaves behind in the imaginations and actions of communities go unaddressed, often with profoundly devastating consequences."

reaching out will involve the demanding work of creating a congregational culture that expresses solidarity and renewal to the shamed, and to the shamer forgiveness and the call to amendment of life.[26]

To this point Braithwaite's work on reintegration may be helpful. He surveys how various societies reintegrate persons who have committed criminal acts. He makes the point that "potent shaming directed at offenders is the essential necessary condition for low crime rates. Yet shaming can be counterproductive if it is disintegrating rather than reintegrating." Shaming is counterproductive when it "leads to stigmatization—to outcasting, to confirmation of a deviant master status." Shaming controls crime when it is "reintegrative, when a community shames while maintaining bonds of respect or love, when a community sharply terminates disapproval with forgiveness, instead of amplifying deviance by progressively casting the deviant out."[27]

Communitarianism is foundational to reintegration and is comprised of three elements: "(1) densely enmeshed interdependency, where the interdependencies are characterized by (2) mutual obligation and trust, and (3) are interpreted as a matter of group loyalty rather than individual convenience."[28] Braithwaite specifically calls out the church as a place of nurture for the reintegration of the shamer where it may be made clear "that even though the blow to reputation has been severe, the offender is forgiven and still accepted by her loved ones, and her loved ones are by her side to provide practical support in getting on with life."[29] Braithwaite's work provides helpful avenues into the pastoral care of the congregation and community under attack by those who would betray its trust and the betrayers of that trust.

There is another important aspect of the pastoral response to theological shame in the context of community. It is the community's power located in its history and its thick web of relationships to act as a restraint upon the one shamed from being persuaded to abandon the God in whom the shamed one has lost faith. In chapter 2, we saw how the pivotal role of Ps 73:15 highlighted the power of community to thwart the tragic outcome of shame's burden.

---

26. See Albers' remarks on the community as healing agent in *Shame: A Faith Perspective*, 129–33.

27. Braithwaite, *Crime, Shame, and Reintegration*, 4, 12–13.

28. Ibid., 86.

29. Ibid., 87.

The Self-Shamed God Who Reconciles

> If I had said, "I will talk on in this way,"
> I would have been untrue to the circle of your children.

The tug of the "circle of your children" still holds when trust in God proves ill founded. Against the force of shame that pushes the speaker's feet to slip and stumble, a more powerful vector is responsibility and obligation to those "who trust me".

The role of pastors in nurturing a community that provides motivation to remain engaged with God even when feeling the shame of being let down cannot be emphasized enough. Psalm 73 wisely places the considerable weight of the community's claims right at the center of a meditation cast otherwise in the terms of a monologue. Even though the speaker wants us to hear about what has happened to him/her, the speaker is not finally at the center of the witness; rather it is the "circle of thy [God's] children." It is the power of this circle which draws the shamed one back into the sanctuary where resolution happens. Pastors will effectively care for the shamed by leading the community to keep the shamed one inside the community's circle of power. By bringing the community into play, pastors will be acting out of the story of the fractured Trinitarian family of God and the role of the Spirit who keeps the Father and the Son in union even in their mutual shame and calls them to new life.[30]

Jones[31] provides several test cases of the community's power to embrace those betrayed with nurture and structure. These range from an inner-city support group for an abused teen-aged girl to the national shock of 9/11 to a support group for women who have experienced miscarriage in pregnancy. She addresses both the challenges and the blessings associated with the support of those shamed by the community. She interprets Calvin's Commentary on the Psalms as his sustained exposition of God addressing the shame of betrayal, and this informs her insight that recovery of damaged imaginations is mediated through the congregation's embodiment of God's grace.

Living Beyond Shame and Worship

When God acts to restore a fractured relationship with a believer who has experienced the shame of ill founded trust, that action is for the sake

---

30. See Billman, "Pastoral Care as an Art of Community," 10–36.

31. *Trauma and Grace*. See also the analysis of the community as a place where structural violence can be healed through the practice of nonviolence in Hess, *Sites of Violence, Sites of Grace*.

The Self-Shaming God Who Reconciles

of upholding the validity of the two-ways formula of living. The classical statement of this formula occurs in Ps 1:6 "For the Lord knows the way of the righteous, but the way of the wicked will perish." Because God has backstopped this formula with God's integrity, God's restorative action is fundamentally for the sake of upholding God's sovereignty.

The action of God is described in both testaments, positively as the saving of the shamed, and, negatively, as the shaming of the opponents of the shamed person. Our study of the fractured Trinity at the event of Jesus' crucifixion and burial uncovered the mystery of the self-shaming God and highlighted the Easter role of the Spirit in bringing both Father and Son back from shame. Because the Trinitarian family of God has taken unto itself shame and found a way to live beyond it, this establishes an unlimited possibility for the reclaiming of both the shamed and the shamer.

In the Bible the locus of the saving of the shamed typically is the place of worship. Our study has examined several liturgical settings: the role the sanctuary played in Ps 73 in restoring trust in God, the liturgy of Joel 2:12–17 concluding with God's promise not to put God's people to shame (2:26–27), the desperate prayers of the people of Nineveh, Jesus' eucharistic lifting of the veil of shame from the travelers to Emmaus, and, by extension, the confession of a deep spiritual bond between the imprisoned Paul and Jesus. We will focus on the liturgical setting Ps 73 affords as the basis of drawing implications for living beyond shame and worship.

In Ps 73 the betrayed one speaks of existential shame, accusing God of a stunning failure. The accusation is caught up and held within the space of prayer, addressed to the very one who is called the betrayer. This accusation is voiced in the sanctuary, in the liturgy. The liturgy comprises two movements (1) "history reduced to its sacred core and its ritual actualization of the past" and (2) "prolepsis, its 'preview' of the future."[32] This suggests that the liturgy acts to restore trust within the shamed one by inviting a recollection of what is immemorial.

The constant response from those who live now beyond shame is praise to the self-shaming God who reconciles. Drawing from the biblical materials in this study, we see praise welling up from several sources.

1. A significant indicator of release from theological shame in the Psalms is the return of speech, specifically of praise to God. In a rare moment of retrospection, the speaker in Ps 73 noted that in the depths of shame the speaker was more like a beast, stupid and ignorant (v. 22). Studies

---

32 Ricoeur, "Lamentation as Prayer," 218.

of extreme suffering often highlight the reduction to speechlessness as a result.[33] Having the ability again to speak indicates that one has moved out of the realm of the sub-human into new life.

2. In Ps 73:21–25 praise issues forth out of a new view of the self. To recall discussion in chapter 2, in the throes of shame (soul embittered and heart pricked) the speaker had become stupid, ignorant and like a beast before God. Yet, despite this descent into sub-human and froward behavior, the speaker had an intimate experience of God's continued faithfulness into the future. This disparity of experience—retrospective negative self-evaluation coincident with a sense of divine faithfulness—became integrated into the self of the speaker through the dimension of awe or praise. "Whom have I in heaven but you? And there is nothing on earth that I desire other than you." Praise is the linguistic clue that the speaker has passed out of the realm of shame and returned to the state of nearness to the goodness of God.

3. Psalm 75 begins and ends with praise that is brought forth by the majestic declaration of God to judge with equity and to steady the earth's tottering pillars. The effect of such judgment is to reaffirm the validity of the two-ways formula of living. Here, as in Ps 73 also, the restatement of that formula at the close of the psalm is attended with the language of praise.

4. Psalm 74 contains language that praises God, recounting all God's wondrous acts in the creation story. Yet here, in a twist of irony, such praise serves to hector God into renewed acts of saving in the situation where the place of praise, the sanctuary, has been demolished.

5. Paul's language of boasting in the Lord transforms the excesses of those who were boasting in themselves into the act of boasting of God's costly work of bringing new life out of death.

6. Habakkuk paints a significant picture of counter-intuitive faith in 3:17–19 that rejoices in time of shame because "God, the Lord, is my strength."

The act of praise coordinates several dimensions of the witness to the self-shaming God who reconciles. Praise indicates that the paralyzing burden of shame is released. Praise voices confidence in and recommitment to

---

33. See n. 17, and Serene Jones, "Emmaus Witnessing," 118.

The Self-Shaming God Who Reconciles

God's sovereign way with the world. As praise celebrates the reasserting of the two-ways formula, praise establishes the foundation for ethics.

Pastors will always be alive to instances of deep and searching awareness of the self that occur as the result of going through an opening to life beyond shame. These moments of awareness ought to be celebrated with praise. In fact, the inclusion of words of awe and praise in Ps 73 (a highly reflective and introspective psalm) permit it to appeal to the entire person—body, mind and spirit.

Pastors will also be alive to the magnificent sweep of God's actions to open a way to live beyond shame. They will share the multifaceted story of God's saving work, and they will lead their congregations in designing worship that is full of the awe and grandeur of the work of God. The Bible shows that worship which helps recall history that is reduced to its sacred core and worship that dramatizes a preview of the future victory will be an instrument of God's saving of the shamed.[34]

Lewis picks up on this transition from silence to speech in his treatment of the shape of the Christian life and the witness of the Church: "Out of the awful, atheistic silence of the first Easter Saturday there burst forth God's death defeating word of resurrection joy and victory. The terminal hush of unanswered questions and sepulchral speechlessness became the ultimate word-event, the rebirth of language in its triumphal and liberating truthfulness . . . The Easter Saturday church, the earthly form now of the incarnate, crucified and risen Word, and filled with the loquacious, pentecostal Spirit . . . has prophetic voice . . . and the command, authority, and power of God to give it utterance."[35]

Finding its voice again, the Church is able to fulfill its vocation as prophet and pastor in service to the eschatological vision of the triumph of God over death. This service takes the bipolar forms of resistance against the forces of death and becoming a presence that betokens new life in settings of death's apparent triumph.[36]

---

34. See the important collection of healing liturgies collected by Evans, *Healing Liturgies*, especially sections on domestic violence and sexual abuse (190–218), criminal justice (377–82), and community reconciliation (397–434).

35. Lewis, *Between Cross and Resurrection*, 373–74.

36. Ibid., 426. "The Friday wail of Christ's forsakenness, and his descent to hell on Saturday, provide our final reassurance that God cries out with us in our abandonment to the tyranny of evil, and will go to any lengths that all things and all persons might be delivered from captivity to death."

This insistence of God's final victory resounds with the Psalter's insistence on God's confirming the validity of the "two ways" of living by vindicating the righteous, righting wrong, and joining with the shamer in bearing judgment so that the shamer may hear the call of mercy.

Conclusion

Implications for Ministerial Formation

This book has been written from the perspective that the church engages in authentic, distinctive witness to the victory of God in Jesus Christ when ministry is built upon a solid biblical and theological foundation. Not only does this foundation support ministry that conveys the distinctive word of God's grace and judgment, but biblical and theological grounding gives the church the *discrimen,* the set of criteria, to engage the world in conversation and action.

To those who confess the Bible to be the rule of faith and doctrine, the question is inescapable: How best to access the Bible as a theological document for the church? We believe that the arc this book traverses, beginning with close reading of texts and passing these results through canonical synthesis and theological matrix, gives promise of opening up the richness of the Bible for the church's faithful witness.

Ministry that integrates biblical study, theological reflection, and practical expression requires the use of the skills of association, imagination and synthesis by leaders who are shaped to view life from a holistic perspective.[1] The church has established seminaries and university based divinity schools for the formation of such leaders. However, the performance of these institutions against the church's expectation has been spotty and uneven. The reasons for this are well known and have received sustained theological reflection over recent decades[2]: the compartmentalization of theological

---

1. Dykstra coined the phrase "pastoral imagination" to signify a distinctive way of seeing and thinking that permeates and shapes clergy practice. See his "The Pastoral Imagination," 1–2, 15. See also the study from the Carnegie Foundation for the Advancement of Teaching, Foster, *Educating Clergy,* 1–16. This study has profited from Kelsey's pioneering investigation of theological education contained in two books, *Between Athens and Berlin,* and *To Understand God Truly.*

2. For an account of the rise of specialization and compartmentalization in theological education, see Farley, *Theologia.*

Implications for Ministerial Formation

disciplines, the pressure of professional guilds on professors to produce technical scholarship, the tenuous ties of institutions and professors to the life of the local congregation, to name the most familiar.[3] This book's inner logic is a plea for renewed attention to a model of pastoral formation that integrates the various departments of graduate theological education to serve primarily the needs of congregations to thrive under the challenges of the twenty-first century.[4] This plea revives classical models of the interplay between scholarship and church pursued, for example, by ancient church fathers and mothers and the Reformers.[5] This model brings significant, new expectations for seminary educators and ministerial students.

---

3. As Sullivan points out in his Introduction to Foster's *Educating Clergy*, 3–4, these reasons are traced to a definition of what is a profession made popular by Talcott Parsons in *International Encyclopedia of the Social Sciences* . Parsons defined a profession by its exercise of "cognitive rationality" seen most clearly in the research university. Sullivan describes how this impacted clergy education and educators.

4. Sullivan, *Educating Clergy*, 7. He uses the phrase "normative apprenticeship" to define the formation of professional identity, 6, 10. Kelsey, *Between Athens and Berlin*, 6–26 uses the terms Athens and Berlin to denominate two opposed models of education. Generally speaking, Athens, with its ties to the practice in Greece of *paideia*, stands for an education that prizes the passing on of a normative tradition from one generation to the next. Berlin, with its ties to the founding of the University of Berlin in the 18th century, stands for dispassionate, value-neutral inquiry. Historically, theological schools have made various compromises and arrangements between the competing influences of these two ways of education.

The field of biblical studies separated higher-critical studies which seek to find meaning "behind" the text (Berlin) from biblical theology or the "message" of the text (Athens). Various theological moves were required to relate the scientific results to the message. A canonical understanding of Scripture seeks to circumvent the need for compromise. This understanding begins with the premise of Scripture already prepared as a theological document. It is the task of canonical criticism to describe the way the ancient interpreters shaped and structured the text to create its final form as Scripture. Though a long process of interpretation, the text has become sufficiently unhinged from history to become a medium of revelation which is accessed with the tools of literary criticism, liturgical sensitivity and devotional practice, for example the classical *lectio divina*. The results of such study are then rarified through a theological conversation and subsequently imaginatively rendered by a community of faith into fruits of ministry. For a recent proposal on rethinking the teaching of the Bible in seminaries and divinity schools, see Martin, *Pedagogy of the Bible: An Analysis and Proposal*.

5. Early on, Childs drew attention to the historical connections in "Recovering an Exegetical Tradition" a chapter in *Biblical Theology in Crisis*, 139–48. For another example of the interplay between higher criticism and nineteenth-century theology that interpreted successfully critical study of Scripture to the English speaking church see Bailey, "Theology and Criticism in William Robertson Smith," and "Authority to Edify," 87–98.

Under this model, persons charged with formation of pastoral leaders would be required to have facility not only in their field of primary expertise, but also to show competency in a complementary field. Scholarly contributions would demonstrate how the integration of fields contributes to the health and vitality of congregational life, as well as the self-care and creativity of the pastoral leader. As clergy educators will be the immediate modelers for seminarians of how to create an integrative ministry, seminary and divinity school professors must acknowledge their calling to be bi-vocational in outlook and language. For example, they would pursue graduate education at the highest level that values and provides cross-training and interdisciplinary experience. Other opportunities for acquiring and maintaining complementary competencies would include post-doctoral and sabbatical settings and professional work outside the classroom.

The implications of the shaping of seminary and divinity school professors go further than attaining and integrating competencies in more than one field. If one's calling is to participate in the formation of pastoral leaders, teachers need to gain experience in the hard work of creating forms of ministry that correspond to convictions born of thought.[6] Most likely this would happen in the context of a congregation that is led by a mature and energetic pastor. Pastoral educators should expect to find their set of teaching skills enhanced from spending a sabbatical or summer in a congregation as theologian-in-residence, pastoral consultant or temporary pastor. With a congregation they could imagine, engage, construct, implement and evaluate paths which render convictions into deliverable experiences of grace and judgment. Such observations would become important insights to be folded into future classroom investigations of the arc of biblical study, theological reflection and unfolding ministry.

The shaping of men and women who are highly qualified practitioners of integrated pastoral formation is incremental. Academic deans would pair junior faculty with seasoned colleagues as teachers and mentors. Team teaching, faculty seminars, and retreats are settings wherein the spirit and skills of this specialized education can be transmitted.

This model of pastoral formation has huge implications for shaping the curricula of seminaries and university based divinity schools. While the specific array of courses and their sequencing would vary across institutions, a common ingredient would be opportunities at every stage for

---

6. Kelsey has made compelling case for the congregation as the central place to practice theology. See his *To Understand God Truly*, 131–60.

students to practice the merging of discrete disciplines and the rendering of ministry initiatives from that merger. Capstone courses, advanced seminars, intern years, theological reflection groups, and pastoral residencies are opportunities to shape ministerial character and sharpen leadership skills under the supervision of proven mentors. At the completion of a Master of Divinity degree, a process could be ingrained that internally guides professional church leaders, and this internal compass should be strengthened throughout one's career through formal and informal continuing education, post-graduate education and peer-to-peer accountability and support groups.

The challenges to leadership of churches in the 21st century will come from all sides of life. One report of a recent high-level consultation of the Presbyterian Church (U.S.A.) began with this preamble:

> We find ourselves in the midst of monumental change in this country and throughout the world. Breathtaking technical advances are influencing how we interact with others, obtain information, and structure our lives. Shifting demographics are reshaping homogeneous neighborhoods into multicultural communities. Tumbling economies are erasing job security and impacting individuals and families in critical, perhaps permanent, ways in areas such as housing and healthcare. Environmental concerns and catastrophes are compelling us to reconsider our patterns of consumption. The world order itself is feeling seismic shifts as popular uprisings challenge and even topple longstanding governments.
>
> Being in the world, the church—especially in North America—finds itself in the midst of these changes. Its position of being a "given" in society evaporated, the church is one of several institutions whose relevance has diminished. Seekers are replacing joiners; the "spiritual" are outnumbering the "religious." Membership and giving are down, leaving an increasing number of congregations without the resources to support a full-time, installed pastor. The growing presence of different cultures and languages in every community in the country is impacting how we do mission and ministry.[7]

The position of this book is that the Bible when it is used as a theological document will provide helpful guidance in meeting these challenges as the history of God's people shows it has done before.

---

7. Six-Agency Leadership Initiative Consultation, PCUSA, February 9–11, 2011.

Bibliography

Aageson, James W. "The Pastoral Epistles, Apostolic Authority, and the Development of the Pauline Scriptures." In *The Pauline Canon*, edited by Stanley E. Porter, 5-26. Pauline Studies 1. Leiden: Brill, 2004.

Albers, Robert H. *Shame: A Faith Perspective*. New York: Haworth Pastoral, 1995.

Alter, Robert. *The David Story: A Translation with Commentary of 1 and 2 Samuel*. New York: Norton, 1999.

Auffret, Pierre. "Essai sur la Structure Litterarie du Psaume 74." *Vetus Testamentum* 33 (1983) 129-48.

———. "Et moi sans cesse avec toi: Étude Structurelle du Psaume 73." *Scandinavian Journal of the Old Testament* 9 (1995) 241-76.

Bailey, Warner M. "Authority to Edify: Verification of Biblical Truth in William Robertson Smith's *Prophets of Israel*." In *Thus Says the Lord: Essays on the Former and Latter Prophets in Honor of Robert R. Wilson*, edited by John J. Ahn and Stephen L. Cook, 87-98. Library of Hebrew Bible/Old Testament Studies 502. London: T. & T. Clark, 2009.

———. "Theology and Criticism in William Robertson Smith." PhD diss., Yale University, 1970.

Balentine, Samuel E. *Prayer in the Hebrew Bible: The Drama of Divine-Human Dialogue*. Overtures to Biblical Theology. Minneapolis: Fortress, 1993.

Barth, Karl. *The Epistle to the Romans*. 6th ed. London: Oxford University Press, 1933.

Barth, Marcus. *Ephesians*. Anchor Bible 34. Garden City, NY: Doubleday, 1974.

Bauckham, Richard. *God Crucified: Monotheism and Christology in the New Testament*. Grand Rapids: Eerdmans, 1999.

———. "God's Self-Identification with the Godforsaken: Exegesis and Theology." In *Jesus and the God of Israel*, 254-68. Grand Rapids: Eerdmans, 2008.

Beare, Francis Wright. *The Gospel according to Matthew*. San Francisco: Harper & Row, 1981.

Berlin, Adele. *Zephaniah*. Anchor Bible 25A. New York: Doubleday, 1994.

Berry, Donald K. "Malachi's Dual Design: The Close of the Canon and What Comes Afterward." In *Forming Prophetic Literature: Essays on Isaiah and the Twelve in Honor of John D. W. Watts,* edited by James W. Watts and Paul R. House, 269-302. Journal for the Study of the Old Testament Supplements 235. Sheffield: Sheffield Academic, 1996.

Billman, Kathleen D. "Pastoral Care as an Art of Community." In *The Arts of Ministry: Feminist-Womanist Approaches*, edited by Christie Cozad Neuger, 10-36. Louisville: Westminster John Knox, 1966.

Billman, Kathleen D., and Daniel L. Migliore. *Rachel's Cry: Prayer of Lament and the Rebirth of Hope*. Cleveland: United Church Press, 1999.

Bibliography

Blumenthal, David R. *Facing the Abusing God: A Theology of Protest.* Louisville: Westminster John Knox, 1993.

Bosman, J. P. "The Paradoxical Presence of Exodus 34:6-7 in the Book of the Twelve." *Scriptura* 87 (2004) 233-43.

Braaten, Laurie J. "God Sows: Hosea's Land Theme in the Book of the Twelve." In *Thematic Threads in the Book of the Twelve*, edited by Paul L. Redditt and Aaron Schart, 104-32. Beihefte zur Zeitschrift für die alttestamentliche Wissenschaft 325. Berlin: de Gruyter, 2003.

Braithwaite, John. *Crime, Shame and Reintegration.* Cambridge: Cambridge University Press, 1989.

Brown, Raymond E. *The Birth of the Messiah.* Garden City, NY: Doubleday, 1979.

———. *The Death of the Messiah: From Gethsemane to the Grave: A Commentary on the Passion Narratives in the Four Gospels.* Vol. 2. New York: Doubleday, 1994.

Brown, Sally A. and Patrick D. Miller. *Lament: Reclaiming Practices in Pulpit, Pew, and Public Square.* Louisville: Westminster John Knox, 2005.

Broyles, Craig C. *The Conflict of Faith and Experience in the Psalms: A Form-Critical and Theological Study.* JSOTSup 52. Sheffield: Sheffield Academic, 1989.

Brueggemann, Walter. "Bounded by Obedience and Praise: The Psalms as Canon." *Journal for the Study of the Old Testament* 50 (1991) 80-91.

———. *A Commentary on Jeremiah: Exile & Homecoming.* Grand Rapids: Eerdmans, 1998.

———. "The Cunning Little Secret of Certitude: On the First 'Great Commandment.'" *Church and Society* 87 (1997) 63-80.

———. "The Formfulness of Grief." In *The Psalms and the Life of Faith*, edited by Patrick D. Miller Jr., 84-97. Minneapolis: Fortress, 1995.

———. "Psalms and the Life of Faith: A Suggested Typology of Function." *Journal for the Study of the Old Testament* 17 (1980) 3-32.

———. "The Psalms in Theological Use: On Incommensurability and Mutuality." In *The Book of Psalms: Composition and Reception*, edited by Peter W. Flint and Patrick D. Miller Jr., 581-602. Vetus Testamentum Supplements 99. Leiden: Brill, 2005.

———. "Reservoirs of Unreason." *Reformed Liturgy and Music* 17 (1983) 99-104.

———. "A Shattered Transcendence: Exile and Restoration." In *Biblical Theology: Problems and Perspectives*, edited by Steven J. Kraftchick et al., 169-82. Nashville: Abingdon, 1995.

———. "A Text that Redescribes." In *The Word that Redescribes the World: The Bible and Discipleship*, edited by Patrick D. Miller Jr., 3-19. Minneapolis: Fortress, 2006.

———. *Theology of the Old Testament: Testimony, Dispute, Advocacy.* Minneapolis: Fortress, 1997.

———. "The Third World of Evangelical Imagination." In *Interpretation and Obedience: From Faithful Reading to Faithful Living*, 9-27. Minneapolis: Fortress, 1991.

———. "Voices of the Night—Against Justice." In *To Act Justly, Love Tenderly, Walk Humbly: An Agenda for Ministers*, 5-28. New York: Paulist, 1986.

Bruegemann, Walter, and Patrick D. Miller Jr. "Psalm 73 as a Canonical Marker." *Journal for the Study of the Old Testament* 72 (1996) 45-56.

Calvin, John. *Commentaries on the Twelve Minor Prophets.* Vol. 15. Grand Rapids: Baker, 1981.

Camp, Claudia V. "The Wise Women of 2 Samuel: A Role Model for Women in Early Israel?" *Catholic Biblical Quarterly* 43 (1981) 14-29.

Bibliography

Campbell, John McLeod. *The Nature of Atonement*. 2nd ed. Grand Rapids: Eerdmans, 1996.

Capps, Donald. *Biblical Approaches to Pastoral Counseling*. Philadelphia: Westminster, 1981.

———. *The Depleted Self, Sin in a Narcissistic Age*. Minneapolis: Fortress, 1993.

Carr, David. *The Erotic Word: Sexuality, Spirituality, and the Bible*. Oxford: Oxford University Press, 2003.

Carroll, Robert P. *Jeremiah: A Commentary*. Old Testament Library. Philadelphia: Westminster, 1986.

Childs, Brevard S. *Biblical Theology in Crisis*. Philadelphia: Westminster, 1970.

———. *The Church's Guide for Reading Paul: The Canonical Shaping of the Pauline Corpus*. Grand Rapids: Eerdmans, 2008.

———. *Introduction of the Old Testament as Scripture*. Philadelphia: Fortress, 1979.

———. *Isaiah*. Old Testament Library. Louisville: Westminster John Knox, 2001.

———. "Reflections on the Modern Study of the Psalms." In *Magnalia Dei: The Mighty Acts of God: Essays in Memory of G. Ernest Wright*, edited by Frank Moore Cross et al., 377–88. Garden City, NY: Doubleday, 1976.

Clifford, Richard J. "Psalm 89: A Lament Over the Davidic Ruler's Continued Failure." *Harvard Theological Review* 73 (1980) 35–47.

Cole, Robert L. *The Shape and Message of Book III (Psalms 73–89)*. Journal for the Study of the Old Testament Supplements 307. Sheffield: Sheffield Academic, 2000.

Conrad, Edgar W. *Reading the Latter Prophets: Toward a New Canonical Criticism*. London: T. & T. Clark, 2003.

Conzelmann, Hans. *Acts of the Apostles*. Translated by James Limburg et al. Hermenia. Philadelphia: Fortress, 1987.

———. *1 Corinthians: A Commentary on the First Epistle to the Corinthians*. Translated by James W. Leitch. Hermeneia. Philadelphia: Fortress, 1975.

Cooper, Alan. "In Praise of Divine Caprice: The Significance of the Book of Jonah." In *Among the Prophets: Language, Image and Structure in the Prophetic Writings*, edited by Philip R. Davies and David J. A. Clines, 144–92. Journal for the Study of the Old Testament Supplements 144. Sheffield: Sheffield Academic, 1993.

Cooper-White, Pamela. *The Cry of Tamar: Violence against Women and the Church's Response*. Minneapolis: Fortress, 1995.

Craig, Kenneth M., Jr. "Interrogatives in Haggai-Zechariah: A Literary Thread?" In *Forming Prophetic Literature: Essays on Isaiah and the Twelve in Honor of John D. W. Watts*, edited by James W. Watts and Paul R. House, 224–44. Journal for the Study of the Old Testament Supplements 235. Sheffield: Sheffield Academic, 1996.

Crenshaw, James L. "A Liturgy of Wasted Opportunity: Am 4:6–12; Isa 9:7—10:4." In *Semitics* Vol. 1, edited by I. H. Eybers and J. J. Glück, 27–37. Pretoria: University of South Africa, 1971.

———. "Theodicy in the Book of the Twelve." In *Thematic Threads in the Book of the Twelve*, edited by Paul L. Redditt and Aaron Schart, 175–91. Beihefte zur Zeitschrift für die alttestamentliche Wissenschaft 325. Berlin: de Gruyter, 2003.

Cross, F. L., and E. A. Livingstone, editors. *The Oxford Dictionary of the Christian Church*. 2nd ed. Oxford: Oxford University Press, 1974.

Daube, David. "Shame Culture in Luke." In *Paul and Paulinism: Essays in Honor of C. K. Barrett*, edited by Morna D. Hooker and Stephen G. Wilson, 335–72. London: SPCK, 1982.

Bibliography

deClaissé-Walford, Nancy L. "An Intertextual Reading of Psalms 22, 23, and 24." In *The Book of Psalms: Composition and Reception*, edited by Peter W. Flint and Patrick D. Miller Jr., 139–52. Vetus Testamentum Supplements 99. Leiden: Brill, 2005.

Deist, Ferdinand E. "Parallels and Reinterpretation in the Book of Joel: A Theology of the Yom Yahweh?" In *Text and Context: Old Testament and Semitic Studies for F. C. Fensham*, edited by W. Claassen, 63–79. Sheffield: JSOT Press, 1988.

Dentan, Robert C. "Literary Affinities of Exodus XXXIV 6f." *Vetus Testamentum* 13 (1963) 34–51.

Dibelius, Martin, and Hans Conzelmann. *The Pastoral Epistles*. Translated by Philip Buttolph and Adela Yarbro. Hermeneia. Philadelphia: Fortress, 1972.

Dillon, Richard J. *From Eye-Witnesses to Ministers of the Word*. Rome: Biblical Institute, 1978.

Dozeman, Thomas B. "Inner-biblical Interpretation of Yahweh's Gracious and Compassionate Character." *Journal of Biblical Literature* 108 (1989) 207–23.

Duff, Nancy J. "Recovering Lamentation as a Practice in the Church." In *Lament: Reclaiming Practices in Pulpit, Pew, and Public Square*, edited by Sally A. Brown and Patrick D. Miller Jr., 3–14. Louisville: Westminster John Knox, 2005.

Dunn, James D. G. "The First and Second Letters Timothy and the Letter to Titus." In *The New Interpreter's Bible*, edited by Leander E. Keck, vol. 11. Nashville: Abingdon, 2000.

Dykstra, Craig R. "The Pastoral Imagination." *Initiatives in Religion* 9/1 (2001) 1–2, 15.

Evans, Abigail Rian. *Healing Liturgies for the Seasons of Life*. Louisville: Westminster John Knox, 2004.

Farley, Edward. *Theologia: The Fragmentation and Unity of Theological Education*. Philadelphia: Fortress, 1983.

Fishbane, Michael. "Arm of the Lord: Biblical Myth, Rabbinic Midrash, and the Mystery of History." In *Language, Theology, and the Bible: Essays in Honor of James Barr*, edited by John Barton and Samuel E. Balentine. 271–92. Oxford: Oxford University Press, 1994.

Flam, Gila. *Singing for Survival: Songs of the Lodz Ghetto, 1940–1945*. Urbana: University of Illinois Press, 1992.

Ford, David F. *Christian Wisdom: Desiring God and Learning in Love*. Cambridge: Cambridge University Press, 2007.

Fortune, Marie M. *Is Nothing Sacred? When Sex Invades the Pastoral Relationship*. San Francisco: Harper & Row, 1989.

Foster, Charles R., et al. *Educating Clergy: Teaching Practices and Pastoral Imagination*. San Francisco: Jossey-Bass, 2006.

Freedman, David Noel. "Dinah and Shechem, Tamar and Amnon." *Austin Seminary Bulletin Faculty Edition* 105.2 (1990) 51–63.

Fridrichsen, Anton. "The Apostle and His Message." In *Exegetical Writings*. edited by Chrys C. Caragounis and Tord Fornberg, 232–50. Tübingen: Mohr/Siebeck, 1994.

Gerstenberger, Erhard S. "Psalms in the Book of the Twelve: How Misplaced Are They?" In *Thematic Threads in the Book of the Twelve*, edited by Paul L. Redditt and Aaron Schart, 72–89. Beihefte zur Zeitschrift für die alttestamentliche Wissenschaft 325. Berlin: de Gruyter, 2003.

Gillingham, Susan. "From Liturgy to Prophecy: The Use of Psalmody in Second Temple Judaism." *Catholic Biblical Quarterly* 64 (2002) 470–89.

Glazier-McDonald, Beth. *Malachi: The Divine Messenger*. SBL Dissertation Series 98. Atlanta: Scholars, 1987.

Goldingay, John. "Old Testament Theology and the Canon." *Tyndale Bulletin* 59 (2008) 17–26.

Goulder, Michael D. *The Psalms of Asaph and the Pentateuch: Studies in the Psalter, III*. Journal for the Study of the Old Testament Supplements 233. Sheffield: Sheffield University Press, 1996.

Gray, Mark. "Amnon: A Chip off the Old Block? Rhetorical Strategy in 2 Samuel 13:7–15. The Rape of Tamar and the Humiliation of the Poor." *Journal for the Study of the Old Testament* 77 (1998) 39–54.

Gunkel, Herman, and Joachim Begrich. *Introduction to Psalms: the Genres of the Religious Lyric of Israel*. Translated by James D. Nogalski. Mercer, GA: Mercer University Press, 1998.

Hanson, K. C. "'How Honorable!' 'How Shameful!' A Cultural Analysis of Matthew's Makarisms and Reproaches." *Semeia* 68 (1994[96]) 81–111.

Hengel, Martin. *Crucifixion in the Ancient World and the Folly of the Message of the Cross*. Translated by John Bowden. Philadelphia: Fortress, 1977.

Herman, Judith Lewis. *Trauma and Recovery: The Aftermath of Violence—From Domestic Abuse to Political Terror*. New York: Basic Books, 1992.

Herzfeld, Michael. "Honor and Shame: Problems in the Comparative Analysis of Moral Systems." *Man* 15 (1980) 339–51.

Heschel, Abraham J. *The Prophets: An Introduction*. 2 vols. New York: Harper & Row, 1962.

Hess, Cynthia. *Sites of Violence, Sites of Grace: Christian Nonviolence and the Traumatized Self*. Lanham, MD: Rowman & Littlefield, 2009.

Hillers, Delbert R. *Micah*. Hermeneia. Philadelphia: Fortress, 1984.

———. *Treaty Curses and the Old Testament Prophets*. Biblica et Orientalia 16. Rome: Pontifical Biblical Institute, 1964.

Hooker, Morna D. "Interchange in Christ." *Journal of Theological Studies* n.s.22 (1971) 349–61.

———. "Interchange in Christ and Ethics." *Journal for the Study of the New Testament* 25 (1985) 3–17.

Hossfeld, Frank-Lothar, and Eric Zenger. *Psalmen 101–150*. Herders theologischer Kommentar zum Alten Testament. Freiburg: Herder, 2008.

———. *Psalms 2: A Commentary of Psalms 51–100*. Translated by Linda Maloney. Hermeneia. Philadelphia: Fortress, 2005.

Huber, Lyn Bechtel. "The Biblical Experience of Shame/Shaming: The Social Experience of Shame/Shaming in Biblical Israel in Relation to its Use as a Religious Metaphor." PhD diss., Drew University, 1983.

Jensen, Joseph E. "Psalm 75: Its Poetic Context and Structure." *Catholic Biblical Quarterly* 63 (2001) 416–29.

Jinkins, Michael, and Stephen Breck Reid. "God's Forsakenness: The Cry of Dereliction as an Utterance Within the Trinity." *Horizons In Biblical Theology* 19 (1997) 33–57.

Johnson, Luke Timothy. *The First and Second Letters to Timothy*. Anchor Bible 35A. New York: Doubleday, 2001.

———. "II Timothy and the Polemic against False Teachers: A Re-examination." *Journal of Religious Studies* 6/7 (1978–1979) 1–26.

Bibliography

Jones, Serene. "Emmaus Witnessing: Trauma and the Disordering of the Theological Imagination." *Union Seminary Quarterly Review* 55 (2001) 113–28.

―――. *Trauma and Grace, Theology in a Ruptured World*. Louisville: Westminster John Knox, 2009.

Käsemann, Ernst. *Commentary on Romans*. Translated by Geoffrey W. Bromiley. Grand Rapids: Eerdmans, 1980.

Keck, Leander E. "Justification of the Ungodly and Ethics." In *Rechtfertigung: Festschrift für Ernst Käsemann zum 70. Geburtstag*, edited by Johannes Friedrich et al., 199–209. Tübingen: Mohr/Siebeck, 1976.

Keefe, Alice A. "Rapes of Women/Wars of Men." *Semeia* 61 (1993) 79–97.

Keel, Othmar. *The Symbolism of the Biblical World: Ancient New Eastern Iconography and the Book of Psalms*. New York: Seabury, 1978.

Kelsey, David H. *Between Athens and Berlin: The Theological Education Debate*. Grand Rapids: Eerdmans, 1993.

―――. *Eccentric Existence: A Theological Anthropology*. Louisville: Westminster John Knox, 2009.

―――. *To Understand God Truly: What's Theological about a Theological School*. Louisville: Westminster John Knox, 1992.

Kessler, Rainer. *Micah*. Herders Theologischer Kommentar zum Alten Testament. Freiburg: Herder, 1999.

Lapsley, Jacqueline E. "Shame and Self-Knowledge: The Positive Role of Shame in Ezekiel's View of the Moral Self." In *The Book of Ezekiel: Theological and Anthropological Perspectives*, edited by Margaret S. Odell and John T. Strong, 143–73. Atlanta: Society of Biblical Literature, 2000.

Ledegang, F. "Images of the Church in Origen: the Girdle (Jeremiah 13,1–11)." *Studia Patristica* 17.2 (1982) 907–11.

Levenson, Jon D. "The Temple and the World." *Journal of Religion* 64 (1984) 275–98.

Lewis, Alan. *Between Cross and Resurrection: A Theology of Holy Saturday*. Grand Rapids: Eerdmans, 2001.

―――. "The Theology of Death and the Care of the Dying: Affirmations, Attitudes and Actions." *Insights* 110 (1994) 7–18.

Lindstrom, Fredrik. *Suffering and Sin: Interpretations of Illness in the Individual Complaint Psalms*. Coniectanea biblica: Old Testament Series 37. Stockholm: Almqvist & Wiksell, 1994.

Livingston, David J. *Healing Violent Men: A Model for Christian Communities*. Minneapolis: Fortress, 2002.

Luyten, J. "Psalm 73 and Wisdom." In *Sagesse de l'Ancien Testament*, edited by M. Gilbert, 59–81. Biliotheca Ephemeridum Theologicarum Lovaniensium 51. Paris: Gembloux, 1979.

Malina, Bruce J., and Jerome H. Neyrey. "Honor and Shame in Luke-Acts: Pivotal Values of the Mediterranean World." In *The Social World of Luke-Acts: Models for Interpretation* edited by Jerome H. Neyrey, 25–66. Peabody, MA: Hendrickson, 1991.

Marsh, W. Eugene. "Amnon's Folly." In *Telling the Truth: Preaching about Sexual and Domestic Violence*, edited by John S. McClure and Nancy J. Ramsay, 141–43. Cleveland: United Church Press, 1998.

Martin, Dale B. *Pedagogy of the Bible: An Analysis and Proposal*. Louisville: Westminster John Knox, 2008.

Mays, James Luther. *Amos*. Old Testament Library. Philadelphia: Westminster, 1969.

———. *Micah.* Old Testament Library. Philadelphia: Westminster, 1976.
———. "The Place of the Torah-Psalms in the Psalter." *Journal of Biblical Literature* 106 (1987) 3–12.
———. "The Question of Context in Psalms Interpretation." In *The Shape and Shaping of the Psalter*, edited by J. Clinton McCann Jr., 14–20. Journal for the Study of the Old Testament Supplements 159. Sheffield: JSOT Press, 1993.
McCann, J. Clinton, Jr. "Books I–III and the Editorial Purpose of the Psalter." In *The Shape and Shaping of the Psalter*, edited by J. Clinton McCann Jr., 93–107. Journal for the Study of the Old Testament Supplements 159. Sheffield: JSOT Press, 1993.
———. "Psalm 73: A Microcosm of Old Testament Theology." In *The Listening Heart: Essays in Wisdom and the Psalms in Honor of Roland E. Murphy*, edited by Kenneth Hoglund, 247–57. Journal for the Study of the Old Testament Supplements 58. Sheffield: JSOT Press, 1987.
———. "The Shape of Book I of the Psalter and the Shape of Human Happiness." In *The Book of Psalms: Composition and Reception*, edited by Peter W. Flint and Patrick D. Miller Jr., 341–43. Vetus Testamentum Supplements 99. Leiden: Brill, 2005.
McCarter, P. Kyle Jr. *II Samuel.* Anchor Bible 9. Garden City, NY: Doubleday, 1984.
McKane, William. "Poison, Trial by Ordeal and the Cup of Wrath." *Vetus Testamentum* 30 (1980) 474–92.
McNish, Jill L. *Transforming Shame: A Pastoral Response.* New York: Haworth Pastoral, 2004.
Miller, Patrick D., Jr. "The Beginning of the Psalter." In *The Shape and Shaping of the Psalter*, edited by J. Clinton McCann Jr., 83–92. Journal for the Study of the Old Testament Supplements 159. Sheffield: JSOT Press, 1993.
———. "Heaven's Prisoners: The Lament as Christian Prayer." In *Lament: Reclaiming Practices in Pulpit, Pew, and Public Square*, edited by Sally A. Brown and Patrick D. Miller Jr., 15–26. Louisville: Westminster John Knox, 2005.
———. "Kingship, Torah Obedience and Prayer: The Theology of Psalms 15–24." In *Neue Wege der Psalmenforschung: Festschrift für W. Beyerlin zum 65. Geburtstag*, edited by Klaus Seybold and Erich Zenger, 127–42. Herders Biblische Studien 1. Freiburg: Herder, 1994.
———. "Prayer as Persuasion: The Rhetoric and Intention of Prayer." *Word & World* 13 (1993) 356–62.
———. "The Psalms as a Mediation on the First Commandment." In *The Way of the Lord*, 91–122. Grand Rapids: Eerdmans, 2004.
———. "The Theological Significance of Biblical Poetry." In *Language, Theology, and the Bible: Essays in Honor of James Barr*, edited by John Barton and Samuel E. Balentine, 213–30. Oxford: Oxford University Press, 1994.
———. "Theology from Below." In *The Way of the Lord*, 270–301. Grand Rapids: Eerdmans, 2004.
Mitchell, David C. *The Message of the Psalter: An Eschatological Program in the Book of Psalms.* Sheffield: Sheffield Academic, 1997.
Moessner, David. "Good News for the 'Wilderness Generation': The Death of the Prophet Like Moses according to Luke." In *Good News in History: Essays in Honor of Bo Reicke*, edited by Ed. L. Miller, 1–34. Atlanta: Scholars, 1993.
Moffatt, James. *The Moffatt Translation of the Bible.* London: Hodder & Stoughton, 1934.
Moltmann, Jürgen. "The 'Crucified God': God and the Trinity Today." In *New Questions on God*, edited by Johannes B. Metz, 26–37. New York: Herder & Herder, 1972.

Bibliography

Muraoka, Takamitsu. *Emphatic Words and Structures in Biblical Hebrew.* Leiden: Brill, 1985.

Nasuti, Harry P. "Interpretive Significance of Sequence and Selection in the Book of Psalms." In *The Book of Psalms: Composition and Reception*, edited by Peter W. Flint and Patrick D. Miller Jr., 311–39. Vetus Testamentum Supplements 99. Leiden: Brill, 2005.

———. "The Poetics of Biblical Prophecy: Point of View and Point of Standing in the Prophetic Books." In *Thus Says the Lord: Essays on the Former and Latter Prophets in Honor of Robert R. Wilson*, edited by John J. Ahn and Stephen L. Cook, 99–113. Library of Hebrew Bible/Old Testament Studies 502. London: T. & T. Clark, 2009.

———. *Tradition History and the Psalms of Asaph.* SBL Dissertation Series 88. Atlanta: Scholars, 1988.

Nathanson, Donald L. *Shame and Pride: Affect, Sex, and the Birth of the Self.* New York: Norton, 1992.

Nogalski, James D. "Joel as 'Literary Anchor.'" In *Reading and Hearing the Book of the Twelve*, edited by James D. Nogalski and Marvin A. Sweeney, 91–109. Symposium Series 15. Atlanta: Society of Biblical Literature, 2000.

———. "Recurring Themes in the Book of the Twelve: Creating Points of Contact for a Theological Reading." *Interpretation* 61 (2007) 125–36.

———. "The Redactional Shaping of Nahum 1 for the Book of the Twelve." In *Among the Prophets: Language, Image and Structure in the Prophetic Writings*, edited by Philip R. Davies and David J. A. Clines, 193–202. Journal for the Study of the Old Testament Supplements 144. Sheffield: Sheffield Academic, 1993.

O'Connor, Kathleen M. *The Confessions of Jeremiah: Their Interpretation and Role in Chapters 1–25.* SBL Dissertation Series 94. Atlanta: Scholars, 1988.

Odell, Margaret S. "The Inversion of Shame and Forgiveness in Ezekiel 16:59–63." *Journal for the Study of the Old Testament* 56 (1992) 101–12.

Oglesby, William B., Jr. *Biblical Themes for Pastoral Care.* Nashville: Abingdon, 1980.

Olyan, Saul M. "Honor, Shame, and Covenant Relations in Ancient Israel and Its Environment." *Journal of Biblical Literature* 115 (1996) 201–18.

Park, Samuel. "An Evolving History and Methodology of Pastoral Theology, Care, and Counseling." *Journal of Spirituality in Mental Health* 9 (2006) 5–33.

Penchansky, David. *What Rough Beast? Images of God in the Hebrew Bible.* Louisville: Westminster John Knox, 1999.

Petersen, David L. *Zechariah 9–14 and Malachi: A Commentary.* Old Testament Library. Louisville: Westminster John Knox, 1995.

Poling, James. "Preaching to Perpetrators of Violence." In *Telling the Truth: Preaching about Sexual and Domestic Violence*, edited by John S. McClure and Nancy J. Ramsay, 71–82. Cleveland: United Church Press, 1998.

Presbyterian Church (U.S.A.). "Six-Agency Leadership Initiative Consultation." Dallas, Texas, February 9–11, 2011. Online: http://www.pcusa.org/media/uploads/oga/pdf/dallasmtngfeb11.pdf.

Ramsay, Nancy. "Compassionate Resistance: An Ethic for Pastoral Care and Counseling." *Journal of Pastoral Care* 52 (1998) 217–26.

———. "Confronting Family Violence and Its Spiritual Damage." *Journal of Family Ministry* 20 (2006) 28–40.

———. "Preaching to Survivors of Child Sexual Abuse." In *Telling the Truth: Preaching about Sexual and Domestic Violence*, edited by John S. McClure and Nancy J. Ramsay, 58–70. Cleveland: United Church Press, 1998.

Redditt, Paul L. "The Production and Reading of the Book of the Twelve." In *Reading and Hearing the Book of the Twelve*, edited by James D. Nogalski and Marvin A. Sweeney, 11–33. Symposium Series 15. Atlanta: Society of Biblical Literature, 2000.

———. "Zechariah 9–14, Malachi, and the Redaction of the Book of the Twelve." In *Forming Prophetic Literature: Essays on Isaiah and the Twelve in Honor of John D. W. Watts*, edited by James W. Watts and Paul R. House, 245–68. Journal for the Study of the Old Testament Supplements 235. Sheffield: Sheffield Academic, 1996.

Rendtorff, Rolf. "How to Read the Book of the Twelve as a Theological Unity." In *Reading and Hearing the Book of the Twelve*, edited by James D. Nogalski and Marvin A. Sweeney, 75–87. Symposium Series 15. Atlanta: SBL, 2000.

Ricoeur, Paul. "Lamentation as Prayer." In André LaCocque and Paul Ricoeur, *Thinking Biblically: Exegetical and Hermeneutical Studies*, translated by David Pellauer, 211–34. Chicago: University of Chicago Press, 1998.

Riemann, Paul A. "Dissonant Pieties: John Calvin and the Prayer Psalms of the Psalter." In *Inspired Speech: Prophecy in the Ancient Near East: Essays in Honor of Herbert B. Huffmon*, edited by John Kaltner and Louis Stulman, 354–400. Journal for the Study of the Old Testament Supplements 378. London: T. & T. Clark, 2004.

Rigby, Cynthia L. "Providence and Play." *Insights* 126 (2011) 10–18.

Roberts, J. J. M. "Of Signs, Prophets, and Time Limits: A Note on Psalm 74:9." *Catholic Biblical Quarterly* 39 (1977) 474–81.

Schart, Aaron. "Reconstructing the Redactional History of the Twelve Prophets: Problems and Models." In *Reading and Hearing the Book of the Twelve*, edited by James D. Nogalski and Marvin A. Sweeney, 34–48. Symposium Series 15. Atlanta: SBL, 2000.

Seitz, Christopher. "Canon, Narrative, and the Old Testament's Literal Sense: A Response to John Goldingay, 'Canon and Old Testament Theology.'" *Tyndale Bulletin* 59 (2008) 27–34.

———. "The Canonical Approach and Theological Interpretation." In *Canon and Biblical Interpretation*, edited by Craig Bartholomew et al., 58–108. Grand Rapids: Zondervan, 2006.

———. *The Goodly Fellowship of the Prophets: The Achievement of Association in Canon Formation*. Grand Rapids: Baker Academic, 2009.

———. "On Letting a Text 'Act Like a Man'—The Book of the Twelve: New Horizons for Canonical Reading with Hermeneutical Reflections." *Scottish Bulletin of Evangelical Theology* 22 (2004) 151–72.

———. *Prophecy and Hermeneutics: Toward a New Introduction to the Prophets*. Grand Rapids: Baker Academic, 2007.

———. "What Lesson Will History Teach?" In *"Behind" the Text: History and Biblical Interpretation*, edited by Craig Bartholomew et al., 443–69. Grand Rapids: Zondervan, 2003.

Sharrock, Graeme E. "Psalm 74: A Literary-Structural Analysis." *Andrews University Seminary Studies* 21 (1983) 211–23.

Sheppard, Gerald T. "'Enemies' and the Politics of Prayer in the Book of Psalms." In *The Bible and the Politics of Exegesis*, edited by David Jobling et al., 61–82. Cleveland: Pilgrim, 1991.

Bibliography

———. "Psalms: How Do the Ordinary Words of Women and Men Become God's Word to Me?" In *The Future of the Bible: How to Read a Book that Seems Intent on Reading You*, 49–98. Toronto: United Church, 1990.

———. *Wisdom as a Hermeneutical Construct: A Study in the Sapientializing of the Old Testament*. Beihefte zur Zeitschrift für die alttestamentliche Wissenschaft 151. Berlin: de Gruyter, 1980.

Shiryon, Michael. "Biblical Roots of Literatherapy." *Journal of Psychology and Judaism* 2 (1977) 3–11.

Sills, David L., editor. *International Encyclopedia of the Social Sciences*. Vol. 12. New York: Macmillan, 1968.

Smedes, Lewis B. *Shame and Grace: Healing the Shame We Don't Deserve*. New York: HarperCollins, 1993.

Smith, Mark S. *The Laments of Jeremiah and Their Contexts*. SBL Monograph Series 42. Atlanta: Scholars, 1990.

Sölle, Dorothee. *Suffering*. Translated by Everett R. Kalin. Philadelphia: Fortress, 1975.

Stansell, Gary. "Honor and Shame in the David Narratives." In *Was ist der Mensch . . . ? Beiträge zur Anthropologie des Alten Testaments: Hans Walter Wolff zum 80 Geburtstag*, edited by Frank Crüsemann et al., 94–114. Munich: Kaiser, 1992.

Steck, Odil Hannes. *The Prophetic Books and Their Theological Witness*. Translated by James D. Nogalski. St. Louis: Chalice, 2000.

Stulman, Louis. "Jeremiah as a Polyphonic Response to Suffering." In *Inspired Speech: Prophecy in the Ancient Near East: Essays in Honor of Herbert B. Huffmon*, edited by John Kalter and Louis Stulman, 302–18. Journal for the Study of the Old Testament Supplements 378. London: T. & T. Clark, 2004.

Széles, Mária Eszenyei. *Wrath and Mercy: A Commentary on the Books of Habakkuk and Zephaniah*. Grand Rapids: Eerdmans, 1987.

Tannehill, Robert C. "The Magnificat as Poem." *Journal of Biblical Literature* 93 (1974) 263–75.

———. *The Narrative Unity of Luke-Acts: A Literary Interpretation*. Vol. 2, *The Acts of the Apostles*. Foundations and Facets: New Testament. Minneapolis: Fortress, 1990.

Torunay, Raymond J. "Le Psaume 73: Relectures et Interpretation." *Revue Biblique* 92 (1985) 187–99.

Trible, Phyllis. *Texts of Terror: Literary-Feminist Readings of Biblical Narratives*. Overtures to Biblical Theology. Philadelphia: Fortress, 1984.

van der Kolk, Bessel A., et al., editors. *Traumatic Stress: The Effects of Overwhelming Experience on Mind, Body, and Society*. New York: Guilford, 1996.

Van Leeuwen, Raymond C. "Scribal Wisdom and Theodicy in the Book of the Twelve." In *In Search of Wisdom: Essays in Memory of John G. Gammie*, edited by Leo G. Perdue et al., 31–49. Louisville: Westminster John Knox, 1993.

Vincent, M. A. "The Shape of the Psalter: An Eschatological Dimension?" In *New Heaven and New Earth—Prophecy and the Millennium: Essays in Honor of Anthony Gelston*, edited by P. J. Harland and C. T. R. Hayward, 61–82. Vetus Testamentum 77. Leiden: Brill, 1999.

Weber, Hans-Ruedi. *The Cross: Tradition and Interpretation*. Translated by Elke Jessett. Grand Rapids: Eerdmans, 1978.

Weiss, Meir. *The Bible from Within: The Method of Total Interpretation*. Jerusalem: Magnes, 1984.

Bibliography

Wenham, Gordon. "Towards a Canonical Reading of the Psalms." In *Canon and Biblical Interpretation,* edited by Craig Bartholomew et al., 333–51. Grand Rapids: Zondervan, 2006.

Westermann, Claus. *Joseph: Eleven Bible Studies on Genesis.* Minneapolis: Fortress, 1996.

Williams, Gary Roye. "Frustrated Expectations in Isaiah V 1–7: A Literary Interpretation." *Vetus Testamentum* 35 (1985) 459–65.

Williamson, H. G. M. "Reading the Lament Psalms Backwards." In *A God So Near: Essays in Old Testament Theology in Honor of Patrick D. Miller,* edited by Brent A. Strawn and Nancy R. Bowen, 3–16. Winona Lake, IN: Eisenbrauns, 2003.

Wilson, Gerald H. *The Editing of the Hebrew Psalter.* SBL Dissertation Series 76. Chico, CA: Scholars, 1985.

———. "King, Messiah, and the Reign of God: Revisiting the Royal Psalms and the Shape of the Psalter." In *The Book of Psalms: Composition and Reception,* edited by Peter W. Flint and Patrick D. Miller Jr., 391–406. Vetus Testamentum Supplements 99. Leiden: Brill, 2005.

———. "Shaping the Psalter: A Consideration of Editorial Linkage in the Book of Psalms." In *The Shape and Shaping of the Psalter,* edited by J. Clinton McCann, Jr. Journal for the Study of the Old Testament Supplements 159. Sheffield: JSOT Press, 1993.

———. "The Use of Royal Psalms at the 'Seams' of the Hebrew Psalter." *Journal for the Study of the Old Testament* 35 (1986) 85–94.

Wolff, Hans Walter. *Hosea.* Translated by Gary Stansell. Hermeneia. Philadelphia: Fortress, 1974.

———. *Joel and Amos.* Translated by Waldemar Janzen et al. Hermenia. Philadelphia: Fortress, 1977.

———. "The Unmasking Word: Micah and the Pious Leadership Circles." In *Confontations with Prophets: Discovering the Old Testament's New and Contemporary Significance,* 35–48. Philadelphia: Fortress, 1983.

Zimmerli, Walther. "Zwillingspsalmen." In *Wort, Lied, und Gottespruch: Beiträge zu Psalmen und Propheten, Festschrift für Joseph Ziegler,* edited by Josef Schreiner, 105–12. Forschung zum Bibel 1–2. Wurzburg: Echter, 1972.

www.ingramcontent.com/pod-product-compliance
Lightning Source LLC
Chambersburg PA
CBHW071624170426
43195CB00038B/2115